THE KINGS
OF ATLANTIS AND WISE MEN OF EGYPT

Armen Petrosyan

ARMEN PETROSYAN

All rights reserved by the author. Copyright № 08/2620 of 16th of August 2012

(The historical and esoteric reconstruction)

DEDICATION

Dedicated to the memory of the great humanist and sage Edgar Cayce and our Russian friend atlantologist Alexander Voronin.

ARMEN PETROSYAN

ABOUT THE AUTHOR AND HIS BOOK

The author of this book is a famous Russian documentary film maker Armen Petrosyan. In recent years, millions of people interested in this subject in Russia and abroad watched more than twenty of his films on the topic of mysteries and stories of mystical events. Among his works are the first Russian documentary about Edgar Cayce, "The Mystery of the Egyptian Pyramids", "Technology of the Ancient Gods," "Is the End of the World canceled?", "New Memories of the Future", "The Silence of Pyramids" and many others. The author's series of films under the general title "Trailing the Mystery" is being broadcasted on the TV channel "Rossiya-Kultura" since 2010.

The historical reconstruction of the esoteric "The Heirs of Atlantis" was created on the basis of numerous known and unknown materials: the emerald Tablets of Thoth-Hermes Trismegistus, the Texts of Pyramids, the mythology of the ancient Egyptians as well as the mythology of the Celts and the mythology of the people of Mesoamerica and the East, Plato's dialogues, "readings" by E. Cayce about the history of ancient Egypt and Atlantis, the old and the new esoteric traditions and legends and many other sources. The real historical events in the life of the main characters as well as their names have been reconstructed from the insights of E. Cayce about that distant era which until recently had been considered prehistoric by our science of history. But over the last decade this old concept was changed. Now the antiquity of the Earth civilization is not 6-7 thousand years old officially, but is already twice as much covering the period of flooding of the last island of the legendary Atlantis. In the scenes of trials and initiations of the priests of ancient Egypt the reader will see the depth and true meaning of the majestic aphorisms of Thoth-Hermes. The meaning becomes obvious not by speculative conclusions but by personal experience of the main characters. The scene of helping the soul of a dead child is described on the basis of personal memories of the author, who survived the clinical death in childhood and thus describes what he had witnessed and clearly remembered. The above distinguishes this book from the usual list of novelties and provides it with a long life for many years to come because the intellectuals of all ages always look for answers to the main and eternal questions about the meaning and purpose of human life.

«Memory of the past is a patrol tower from which can clearly be seen the future».

Yeghishe, an Armenian historian, 5th century.

PART 1
THE NILE VALLEY. 10TH MILLENNIUM B.C.

1. The Stars of Egypt

The sun had disappeared behind the horizon and its recent reflections ceased to play in the waves of the river. The birds stopped singing, even the moon did not peep out as if it fell asleep before anyone else. The distant stars lit up and glitter in the vast sky. The four-year boy, fascinated by their splendor, left his toys and went to the balcony. Jerking up his curly head he began to stare at them in amazement. He had never seen such stars before. Maybe it was because of the new moon or because the boy had never been alone with them at nightfall, but the more the child peered into the sky the stronger grew his surprise and admiration. In a moment he realized that the sky is not flat. On the contrary, it is infinitely extended in depth and it appeared as a huge and vast valley. It was clear that some stars are closer to him, while others, on the contrary, peacefully flickered in some distant depths of the universe. But what stroke him the most? This grandiose view resembled the road that goes into the unfathomable distance and that distance seemed to become accessible and close to him. The boy suddenly felt that all the vast cosmos was densely populated. He heard a soft and distant chime of the stars and realized they were all talking to each other. Large and small, far and near, golden, green, with reddish-pink shades, with blue and violet gleam, they had a peaceful and quiet conversation with each other as if they were all one family. The boy saw how their talking rays stretched to each other, mingled with joy and communicated. He was surprised to realize that numberless living entities, countless as the stars themselves, live in these worlds and their rays; they make friends, go to each other's homes, rejoice together, play and sing, all the time doing something. He felt that they all love each other like brothers and sisters and they all feel happy together. Charmed, the kid looked for the first time in his life at the panorama of the Universe. He also wanted to participate in it. He felt as if he found himself at the big and joyful celebration where everyone was busy and not paying attention to him, but at the same time he was welcomed to participate in the overall rejoicing. Silent admiration never left his face. His lips stretched slightly in a blissful smile. He was silent. Finally he remembered that he was a well-bred boy who upon coming into a dazzling and admirable society should at least say hello to all. Therefore he said quietly to himself: 'Hello, Stars ...'

He did not notice that his mother, silently treading barefoot, came to his room and not finding him there went out on the balcony.

'Who are you talking to, Gorik?'

He turned his frozen in rapt contemplation face to his mother and said: 'To them', and he again looked up in the sky. 'To who? To stars?' mother surprised, 'Who taught you this, my boy?'

'Nobody, Mom, I myself... Can't we talk to the stars?'

She came and bent over her son, she embraced him and, lifting his small and light body, gently hugged him.

'You can, my darling... Your grandfather used to talk to stars...'

Hearing about his grandfather, whom he had never seen, but whom he deeply loved by hearing stories about him from parents, the boy revived, averted his eyes from the sky and turned to his mother.

'How did my grandfather talk to them, Mom?' She paused. There was sadness in her eyes.

'One day, during a long drought in all of Egypt even Nile became shallow; its waters became muddy and dirty. People drank this water, and many of them became sick and died. Crops burned out, canals and trees dried up, and famine extended throughout the country. That time, I remember, there was same new moon as now. The stars were big and bright. They seemed close. Grandfather got up on the roof, raised his hands to the sky and said only two words: 'Stars ... send rain...' And in the morning we were awakened by the noise of the shower. The whole sky was overcast, the rain poured down without ceasing for three days. People and animals were jumping in the rain and enjoyed...' 'Mom, when will we go to Grandpa?'

'When?... When you grow up, my boy...'

And the mother tenderly pressed her son's head to her breast so that he could not see a hot tear of her long and inescapable grief. Feeling her mood the boy asked in surprise: 'Mom, why is it that everyone, even the distant stars have seen our grandfather many times but I can only see him when I grow up?'

She sighed sadly and said quietly: 'Probably, my boy, because there are still many cruel people in this world and they are ruthless, even to the righteous. Merciless time that separates loved ones eventually leads them to a new meeting, if not here, then in the other world. We will someday see him...'

So, they remained for some time motionless under the glittering dome, embracing each other and thinking about the one out there who was dear to them. They did not notice how high above their heads, silently slitting the night mist, swept big winged shadows.

2. The Night Battle

Seating with his son in a cockpit of his vimana, the aircraft of Atlantis, Commander Zuluum looked at the panel. Shimmering hemisphere illuminated everything on the ground as if it was the day rather than a moonless night. The villages and small towns below were easily recognizable. He made two circles around terrain and understood everything. He wrinkled his old eyes and turned to his son: 'Chaakun, we will stop here between the two villages. There will be enough of living things.'

The plane hovered in the air and began to land slowly. A dozen of tall and mighty Atlantean warriors rushed to the largest house nearby. Together they broke through the gate with one blow, burst into the house and began to grab sleepy people who were a head shorter than them. The people were bewildered. They had no time to resist. The soldiers hoisted the captives on their shoulders, brought them to viman and then again broke into the next house. Seeing that its inhabitants were dark-skinned, too, Chaakun said to his father, 'Sons of Thevetata pay ten times more for whitefaces, father. Allow me to find them!'

'Find, Chaakun. But be careful, take soldiers with you.'

Chaakun grabbed one of the bound captives and fiercely asked him: 'Where is village of white-faced here?'

The tied captive moved his head into the distance. Chaakun called four of his Atlanteans and they headed toward the distant homes. But when they came to the gate and tried to open it with one blow, they failed. Realizing that the bolt is made not of wood but of metal Chaakun took his rod of lightning and clicked the button on the handle. The green light on the wand switched for the orange one. He aimed the rod into the slot between the gate and pulled the handle. A bright bluish beam flashed and the gate opened. Atlanteans broke into the yard but they were already expected. Chaakun heard the darts whizzed from right and left, and on both sides his soldiers emitted dull moans of pain. He grabbed the wand with his left hand and with the right hand he unfastened his mace. The courtyard was dark and he could not see anything, but he knew that their silhouettes were visible to the enemy. Suddenly he received a heavy blow on his left arm, the rod flew out of it. He waved back with a club into the darkness but the mace went through the void. Realizing that a clever enemy already changed the place he waved the other way but hit only a shield. Again he received an even stronger blow and dropped his club.

Chaakun again heard how, clenching their teeth, his warriors moan, feeling the pain from received blows, and he realized that they should save themselves. He jerkily shouted to his soldiers, 'Retreat!, and they quickly retreated back to their vimana. Having them on board, the ship sore up into the sky. The old Zuluum while the wounded were being bandaged, was looking at their injuries. One warrior had a pierced armor and broken ribs, the other had his thigh pierced almost through, but the bone was not affected. They all had damaged hands and if not for the armor on elbows, they could be left without hands. The old man said to his son: 'They were Aryans. Only they can be so bold. They do not afraid of us even though they are shorter and weaker.' 'It was dark, father, we did not see them at all.'

'You did the right thing by retreating. Had you stayed, they would have killed all of you quickly, or tied you like prisoners.'

Zuluum ordered the pilot: 'Stop vimanas and open the Sushumna. Show me the house where they were injured.'

Viman was hovering in the air. Spherical device lit up with yellow light. The old man looked in it and said, 'Four warrior, two women and one child. It would be good to teach these Aryans, but the City of Sun is nearby in the north. If their watchmen recognize our vimanas, we will have to return the booty.

Ashamed Chaakun lowered his head: 'I dropped my staff there...'

'Silly boaster! See these white-faced slaves! From now on you will be wiser. If they got the lightning rod then they can knock our ship down. Their leaders know how to operate it. Though they have no fire weapons, the children of the Sun taught them how to use it. And now we should fly home and thanks gods of the night we all alive and got our prey.'

Seeng that the enemy left people lit the laps in the courtyard. One of the defenders with a sword in his hand picked up an abandoned club. Little Horus ran up to him with a dart. Seeing the baby father patted his curly head, 'You are a real warrior, my son!,

Another man came up to them. 'You have a glorious heir, Rame! Gods bless him and all of us today! Tell me, brother, how did you learn about the danger and warned me to prepare arms?'

'I was awakened by the distant sound of blow. A few minutes later I heard another one. I looked out the window and saw a light in one of the houses. Then I realized that someone came to the village not for the good.

The small boy weeling around the adults noticed the rod in the grass, he picked it up and began to examine. Turning to his father with a smile he gave it to him. Both men released a cry of surprise, 'Wand of Lightning! That means we were visited by wandering in the night kidnappers!' 'Praise the gods, Razmik, that we did not let the enemy to take us like sheep!' 'Surely the gods always protect sensitive.'

Rame pressed the button on the wand, the red light

went out and the green lit.

3. The Night Council. Peos, the City of Atlantis

Leaders of the twelve most powerful clans of the northern part of Atlantis, who worshiped the gods of the night, gathered in a large and luxurious room. It was night. The wind carried the scent of the sea, rustling the leaves. A light night rain brought coolness. Finally, for the first time in many days and nights the heat has backed off a bit. One of the walls in the hall is lit from above and below. It is a large relief map that shows all the countries of the world, along with the seas and oceans. The oldest, seated on his throne, begins the council, 'Talking animals brought bad news: the gods of the underground fire became restless. Our scouts have told us that the children of sun-gods have already started to send ambassadors to the land of their brothers. They want to remind them of the Big Kings Council's decision. This means they will soon begin to prepare his people for migration. We can stop them, but if the Lords of Storm come to the country of Poseidon, we will also need to find new land for our people. What do you think, gentlemen?

An old man dressed in black with a large decoration of precious stones and gold on his chest gets up, 'If the sons of the sun-gods will move to the east and the west, than we have to go to the south and north. If we find a new safe place and fortify there, then we can continue to fight with them. But if we disturb them now, we will only waste our time. We must outpace them. And may the moon-gods help us!

The oldest says, 'You spoke wisely, Balamantu! Who among you is ready to go and take a foreign land?

An another member of the Council gets up, 'We all love the country of our ancestors, and we don't want to leave it. The other lands are populated only by living savages that are good only as talking things and slaves. But if such is the will of the gods, I am ready to lead my troops to the war!

The oldest asks him, 'Where will you lead your soldiers, Atseoytl?'

Atseoytl comes up to a large relief map on the wall, 'Balamantu is right, I will not go through Mayapan (shows at the Yucatan and the isthmus with Poseidonis), in the valley of the Great River (shows Egypt) to the Gate of the Sun (shows Babylon and the bay), in the land of Myra (pointing to the west of the continent with the present-day states of Nevada and Colorado) and land of fire and metal (pointing to the east of North America), as well as to the shores of a large Middle lake (pointing to the north and south of the Mediterranean). I do not want our enemies to be in our way. So I will go to the northeast (shows British Peninsula). Those who want can go with me.

One by one they all come up to him and put their hands on the map in the showed location. The last one said, 'To go there by the sea will take a few days. Do you have enough ships and vimans, Azeyotl?'

'If you give us yours, we will share booties with you, Tuahell!'

'I'll give you all my 200 ships together with my people. When you land, I will come there also by the vimana.'

They stretch out their hands at the face level, touching each other with the inner part of the palms and then put their hands on the map. The oldest says, 'Your decision is right, Azeyotl. Our enemies will meet with our revenge anyway. We should start to prepare our people. And may the moon-gods help you!'

4. Poseidonis

Although they flew in the night direction, the dawn has still caught them. The smart machine has automatically found a house on the edge of town and gently landed from above directly into the large courtyard. The prisoners were taken out of the Vimana, led to the barn and seated in a circle. Soon the guests appeared despite the early hour. It seemed everything was already settled with them. They came in and along with the owners began to examine and probe the living things. One of them touched the blacks and then wiped his hands with a handkerchief in disgust. The prisoners did not understand their language but they knew how new owners called them: "the living or talking things". Finally inspection ended, the handkerchief was thrown to the ground, the guests pulled out the money and went along with the owner to pay. Tied and depressed captives sat for a long time in silence, trying to figure out what awaits them. Finally the youngest asked, 'Grandpa, they will sell us?'

The gray-haired old man did not answer immediately, 'I was a boy, my grandfather told me that once upon a time, when the desert was not there, our family lived on the coast. And the sea-traders considered their biggest success to get to the land of Aztlan. People of Aztlan were the richest and most generous in the world, they paid for everything with gold and silver according to number or weight of the things.'

The prisoners were surprised and one of them asked, 'Uncle Afteb, according to number or weight of the things? How is that? One-to-one for any product?'

'Yes, Tamil. For a thousand pounds of dry fruits they could give as much silver coins, and for a hundred painted bronze vessels they would give as much gold coins. Whereas here the cost of these things is ten coins at the most. And besides, they had plenty of their own things, too, and merchants from around the world used to come to them in a great number. And yet they did not bargain, but paid at once as much as you would request. And those of our people, who knew well how to get there by sea, only after a few years of going there, could henceforth live in clover and even left something for their children...

'What are you talking about, Dad? They were all so rich and kind? And now Aztlan men sell people of other lands for gold as a commodity! They grab them in the middle of night right out of theirs houses! Oh gods, why did they fall so low?!' 'I do not know, son. You should ask the sages about it. Something in this world have changed dramatically ... 'What do we do now, Grandpa?'

'What can do he, my boy, who cannot escape, and whose hands are tied? We can only pray to the gods and ask them for help ...'

And the old man softly sang a sad old song about how cruel is the fate of a slave, and how painful it is to long for his native land and rely only on the mercy of the gods. Let them hear the pleas of the miserable...

5. A Messenger. The Nile Valley

Little Gor had already fallen asleep in his cradle when Asmini heard the distant sound of horses' hooves. The sound grew quickly, and when it stopped, there was a loud knocking at the gate. She barely had time to go down when she heard her husband's voice in the yard. While she was lighting the lamps, her husband returned to the house along with the arrived messenger.

'Asmin, the Emperor is calling me and Razmik. Lock the gates after we go.'

'Right in the middle of night, Rame? What happened? Is enemy coming?'

'No, honey. Ambassadors came to Pharaoh, but they are ambassadors of peace, not war. And the ruler decided to get all the courtiers and generals together on the urgent council.

While they were talking, Razmik came. He was already in the ceremonial garb and ready to leave. Adjutants in the yard harnessed the chariot. Sleepy Gor got down the stairs from the top and reached his hands to his father. The boy asked the father to take him, 'Dad, I'm coming with you, too.'

The father picked up the kid in his arms, kissed him in the cheek and said, 'Gor, children cannot be on the night council, the other kids are already asleep and you will have no one to play with in the courtyard. In my absence, you should behave like a real man. Can you?

The boy nodded and kissed his father in return. Rame gave his son to his wife, got up to his chariot and gave horses a whip, sending them into the darkness. The servants locked the gate, and the mother with her son in her arms was still standing in the yard until the sound of hooves die away in the distance...

6. The Council at Pharaoh's

Ehe throne room was crowded and noisy. Gathered generals, senior priests and counselors talked to each other quietly and softly, but there were so many of them that the air was filled with the hum. In the far corner sat tall athletic ambassadors wearing unusual for these places and slightly gleaming golden clothes. Pharaoh came out, accompanied by the principal priests and advisers. Having seated on the throne, he said, 'My sons, you all know about the decision of the Earth Kings Council to host those who by the will of the gods are soon to leave their homeland. This night the ambassadors of our brother, the king of Aztlan, have come to us. Gods have revealed to him that he should begin to withdraw his people from the land of Poseidon, for the Lord of the Seas will soon take their beautiful country with its towns and villages.

All present uttered a sigh of astonishment and then went on to listen attentively. The governor continued, 'People of Aztlan will be coming to us, as well as to other kings, our brothers, in their land. But now they will not come in handfuls as before, but in big waves — in many thousands. Their small colony in the north, where they are building the city of Isis and Osiris, cannot accommodate all of them. They will have to build new cities in our land with our help. You know that even my great-grandfather Ararta with my grandfather Araaraart the Great gave their word to the gods at the time of the Council of all the kings. We must carry out the will of the gods and ancestors. I want each one of you, as soon as the night ends, to tell to your kinsmen, friends and subordinates that the white-faced people of Aztlan would live together with us in our land as our brothers. You should tell that they will be as many as us, white-faced and black-faced. Tell that anyone who unfairly raise the hand at one of them or hurt them with cutting word, he will have to answer for himself according to the law of our ancestors. Now let them tell themselves.

Ambassadors came to the throne and bowed respectfully before Pharaoh. Chief among them spoke with solemnity, 'Thank you, the ruler of Egypt, for your faithfulness to the Law of One and the will of the gods!'.

Then he announced to all, 'We've brought the large mirror of Maguses as a gift for the king of Egypt.

The last words caused a stir among the all present, and the ambassador continued, 'You know, brothers, that the people of Astlan are long famous worldwide for their arts to create magic items. Our metal bird vimanas are shining on the sun. They can carry soldiers and fly in the sky much higher and faster than falcons and eagles. The wonders of our mirrors are legendary and known around the world. People have heard from their ancestors that one can see the most distant places and even the past and the future in those mirrors. Through them you can hear with your ears the sound of other people's thoughts even in the most distant countries. Nobody outside of our lands and seas can make such a mirror. Even the mirrors of the countries of Gobi are made by masters of Poseidonis. The fact that we brought it as a gift means, that now it is time of great change. And we are ready to share everything with our brothers in response to their friendship and hospitality.

While the members of the council quietly discussing all this together, the guests brought a gift, put it in a corner so that it could be seen by the king and everyone else, and asked to put out the lamps. As soon as it became halfdark as before the dawn, the mirror came to life and lit up from the inside. It began to show unknown townscapes as if in the bird's-eye view. Chief Ambassador briefly described everything. He spoke about the beautiful and majestic cities of his native country and called their names. No sooner had he started to talk about any details then the magic mirror showed it larger and closer,

'The sunrise side is less populated. There are very few cities. More people live on the side of the sunset. These beautifully painted buildings — our temples built for the gods. The disc of the sun on the wall of the temple we consider the only worthy image of the higher gods. This gold disc was arranged in the time of the construction in such a way so that the first ray of sun would lit it up during the spring equinox or the summer solstice.

And now, my brothers, you see the city of Alta. It is the capital of the Poseidon land. It is made in the same way as the city of the Golden Gate — a great capital of Aztlan, which was covered with the ocean in long past big star cycles of time. It was thousands of years ago, but Alta is as much beautiful as the Golden Gate. The walls of its interior rings emit a fiery brilliance, but they are covered not with gold, but with the native orichalcum, which is only in our land. Others have just copper. This large and beautiful palace was built specifically for visitors from distant lands and countries. And on a high ground in the center of the city is a palace of our master, the king of Aztlan and the lord of turquoise throne. In the middle of the Acropolis is the Temple of Poseidon and Cleito. It is surrounded with the wall made of pure gold and there the covenants of our gods are kept.

What the ambassador said appeared in the mirror. Not far from the sea, a high majestic wall encircled the entire island. The island space behind it was densely built up, and the duct and a large harbor were filled with boats. The entire island was lying quite high with coast in the form of steeply bluffs. From the bluffs to the sea lad beautiful stairs made of blue stone and surrounded by lush vegetation. The city itself was located on a plain surrounded by mountains. Rivers, lakes, meadows, canals, crowded villages — all breathed with prosperity and abundance. The huge city surrounded by mountains and consisting of uniformed strips of land and water, was glittering under the rays of the setting sun. The city with its golden walls and crystalline blue of the splashing waves was sparkling. When mentioned, the palace was zoomed in the mirror. After the hall with the throne of turquoise the Cleito Temple and Poseidon appeared in the mirror. Around them streamed beautiful fountains and pools. Inside the temple was a large Orichalcum stele with hieroglyphs.

Many wanted to know various details, they began to ask lots of questions. Affected and amazed with the greatness of what they saw, when they all ceased to ask questions, the ambassador spoke again to Pharaoh, 'Lord of Egypt, say, what would you like to see yourself?'

The king thought for a moment, and his eyes were sad, 'I wish to see the land of my ancestors, which in my whole life I have seen only once a long time ago, as a child. I'm getting only rare news from there now and do not know how my kinsmen live there.'

'Then, sir, remember the land.'

And as soon as the king closed his eyes, releasing memories from his childhood, a distant mountainous country became visible for all in the mirror. Its appearance caused exclamations of surprise in the room — many heard about it a lot only from their seniors and did not even know the names of those relatives who remained there. Dawn sun was rising over the two-headed mountain shedding the radiant light on a beautiful mountain valley, covered with blossoming greenery and rugged with straight as an arrow channels filled with reflecting water. In the very heart of the valley stood a city with buildings of different shades of red, pink and yellow stone. The city was waking up from a dream. King peered intently as the grand palace was getting more visible in the mirror. He saw a bearded man on the balcony. The man was looking into the courtyard, where the servants saddled horses. Pharaoh came down from his throne and went to the mirror. As if sensing his gaze, the man turned his face to him and peered into the distance, as if trying to see something. The king stood before the mirror, watching right in the eyes of the stranger and whispered,

'Vardan, my dear brother, I saw you only when you were very small and I did not know what you've become now ...'

The man in the mirror was looking at him silently, and his glance emanated a strong yearning. He did not open his mouth, but suddenly everyone clearly heard his voice,

'Arar-rat, my distant brother, how are you doing there, on the throne of our grandfather...?

7. The Ireland. The Fort of Ekoss

Hundreds of arrived ships disembarked thousands of Aztlan soldiers on the bank. Their foremost troops go ahead and enter deep into the land of the alien country. They walk through the woods. The patrols of local residents report to their leaders about the invasion. Soon, the Atlanteans are already battling with the Celts. Celts incur loss and retreat, and new forces from the fortress come to their help. Atlanteans use their rods of lightning, and the Celts again recede. Their leader watches the battle from the tower of his fortress. Releasing lightning bolts, rows of Atlanteans come closer to the fort. Soldiers of the Celts come back into their fortress. Their leader asked the young soldier standing next:

'Kukhulin, you've been in their lands. What kind of weapons these fomorians have?'

'Wands of lightning, my lord. If they come up a hundred steps from the gates, they can burn it, but they are powerless against the walls of stone. Yet in their vimana they have "The Eye of Balor" that can destroy the entire fortress. This weapon is so complex, that it can be triggered only by three or four people. One is regulating the position in the air, the second is holding the target, the third is observing the flow of fire. And the staffs of officers and the eyes of vimanas shoot with the fiery force transmitted through the air from a glass tower, high as a mountain, on their island.'

'What do we do, prince?'

'Until vimanas come we can stop them only with our fiery weapons, otherwise they will break through the fortress. If vimanas come, I will need the Wings of the Wind.'

'It is good that we have managed to build a forge, like in Dundilgan. Command to prepare a rain of fire!'

Kukhulin slightly nodes to the leader and runs to the central tower. In its rear portion the blacksmiths work, inflating bellows. The first ranks of Aztlan soldiers come from the forests. A young man on the tower gives the order to start. Blacksmiths open the drain of furnace, and molten metal flows out in three ditches. It is poured into a stone bowls, which are parts of a large catapult. When only a hundred steps separate the enemy from the fortress,

Kukhulin orders to release the catapult. Celts knock out the locks with hammers and three large fire-rains fly at the approaching Atlanteans. Many of them injured fall to the ground, the others turn and ran back into the forest. The leader of their warriors approaches Atseoytl, who stands on the shore and watches the disembarking, and shows him a piece of cooled metal.

'Lord, half of our warriors are wounded! These broad-headed savages have a rain of fire!'

'They know,' Atseoytl replied, 'how to make it of copper? Well, we will not mutilate our people in vain, we should wait for the battle vimana, Tuahella. Tomorrow at sunset he will be here. And then we will knock them out of their fortress, or even turn it all into a rain of fire, what these savages never dreamed of!'

8. Split

The first ray of sun entered the Seth temple and lit the stern face of the statue of main god for the blacks. A priest, who has been awake all night in front of it, bowed before the stern god in reverence. A few minutes later the stone statue all of a sudden started to hum softly. Priest anxiously looked up and saw some transparent oily liquid dripping from the face of God. Falling on the floor of the sanctuary, drops were getting reddish and looked like blood. Priests were called. They came running and when they heard the growing rumble and saw drops on the statue of the god, they all prostrated before it. The priest ordered the youngest to run for the oldest. The youth rushed down the street of the village to the house of the chief priest. After telling him the news, he ran on to the elder's house. Half an hour later all the inhabitants of the neighboring villages were already at the gates of the temple. The crowd was buzzing like a disturbed hive. Having done all the necessary rituals, the chief priest came to an anxious people: 'Brothers! We begged Seth to reveal his will to us! God is upset because our people are being kidnapped by the people of Aztlan wandering in the night! And the ruler of Egypt announced that these robbers will now live with us!

The crowd erupts with shouts. People wave arms and demand to go to the king. The priests and the elders of the villages lead the rebellious procession. The news of the will of god rapidly spreads throughout the county. On the way, new masses of people from the black villages join them.

A multi-thousand crowd with axes and hoes in the hands fills the square in front of the palace of Pharaoh. Guardians lock the gates. Head guard goes out on the wall and turns to the crowd:

'What brings you here, black brothers?'

'We do not want red-faced to settle here!' the crowd cries, 'People of Aztlan steal our brothers! Wanderers in the night hide in the dark! We will not allow them to come to us in the light of the sun!'

Leaders and priests of blacks go out of crowd. Stopping the cries with gesture, the eldest of them says to the officer: 'Tell Pharaoh that we have come to talk to him!'

The chief ordered to open the gate, and a group of people enters the palace.

9. Pharaoh's Palace

Pharaoh is seated on his throne. The people bowed down.

'What brings you here, my children?'

Senior replies: 'The Emperor! You've ordered to accept Aztlan people in our land. But they are thieves and robbers! They steal our brothers!

The leader points at two peasants who came with him:
'Let these poor workers tell everything. Tell it to the king of Egypt!'

Paupers come forward and bow low to Pharaoh. One of them says:
'Lord of Egypt! On the last night of the new moon slavers came to our village! At dawn, my brother's house was empty, and the gates have been broken! People of Aztlan steal our brothers!

Pharaoh is thoughtfully caressing his beard. The chief commander approaches him:
'O king, these people are telling the truth. Two houses in their village had been abducted — twenty-three people all together. Two of our officers of the squadron "Amon" Razmik and Rame fought with the kidnappers and got the trophy — the lightning rod.

Pharaoh asks indignantly:
'So the Atlanteans dared to attack my sons? Come on, call their ambassadors!'

The commander sends his adjutant and answers:
'They've paid for it, Your Majesty. Five bloody footprints were left on the ground after their escape. Our

valiant soldiers seized two mace and scepter.'

'Rame and Razmik are truly brave warriors. Let them take the trophies. Reward each of them with a talent of gold.'

'Right you are, my lord!'

The king addresses to the quietened farmers:
'Now they will come. I will order them to return your relatives. But you will have to go with them on their island to find our people. Without you, no one will recognize them.'

Farmers fall on their knees:
'Have mercy, sire! They will sell us there as a commodity!'

'These people are my friends. Do not be afraid, they will not hurt you, but rescue your loved ones from captivity and will return you all home. I'll send my most courageous warriors with you. Make up your mind!'

The leader of the black-skinned answers on behalf of all:
'Your Majesty! But if our people do not come back, you will not go to war in the land of Aztlan. And then people will say that you are not only accepting the robbers, but also give our own men to them. What should we do then? Where should we seek protection?'

'My brothers, you should have at least a drop of courage to rescue your people from captivity. If you do not, then what can I do? Should I go there myself? Yes, I would go to save my subjects, but I do not know their faces. How can I find them? Should I ask every slave-trader "Was it you who visited us at the new moon?!"

Decide, otherwise no one will help these poor people.'

'Forgive us, lord! But we do not believe the people of Aztlan. And we do not believe you either. Your soldiers managed to protect their own homes from them, but we could not. Where can we go?'

The face of Pharaoh becomes cold and stern:

'Go and think carefully. I can only demand from their king to return our people. And he will fulfil my will. But without your help, he will just not find them. Go and ask all your villagers. If at least one has the courage to go there and find them, I give you my word that everyone will return safe and sound!'

Dark-skinned bow down and leave the palace. A huge crowd surrounds them and silently listens to the story. However, the fear of red-faced and Pharaoh's order to find those who are ready to go to the island caused a storm of indignation and prevented them from proper understanding of the situation. The crowd begins to scream and throw stones in the direction of the palace. The black priests are trying to stop people, but no one hears. The chief guard orders to lock the gates. But the blacks brought a thick log with them. They drug it by ropes from the far end of the square and start to hit it against the wall. Behind stones off went the arrows, and a real assault on the palace began. The resounding echoes of blows at the gate drown the thousand screams of the crowd. The soldiers on the walls pull their bows. Upon hearing the noise Pharaoh goes out on the wall and stops the solders from shooting down. He climbs the tower and raises his hands, demanding silence from the crowd. Stones and arrows fly at him. The guards barely have time to cover their king with their shields. The rumble of blows at the gates hushed for a minute but then increases with renewed vigor. The gates crack, but yet continue to hold.

The soldiers put logs under them so that they are not collapsed.

The chariot drove into the yard of the house of ambassadors with full speed. The messenger climbs the stairs and tells the strangers that Pharaoh is urgently calling them. He tells about the recent kidnapping and the indignation of the people. The red-faced get in their vimana with delta-shaped wings, which was right there in the yard. Viman rises into the air and smoothly flies at low level to the palace. A minute later, sitting at the console

Atlantian says to the other:
'Brother Iltar, look, there is a real fight!'

'Yes, brother Votan, the sons of Thevetata had succeeded to defame our name here as well! Now Arar-rat must either reject us or punish his people!'

'What do we do? If we are to stand up for the Pharaoh, they will hate us even more.'

'And if they overcome the Aryans by their large number, it will turn out that we have betrayed those who are faithful to our friendship. Open Mash-Mak h very little!

Generals place all warriors of the palace in front of the gates and in towers. The head guard reports to the king that the resin is already in full boiling and it can be poured on attackers. Pharaoh ordered to wait until the gate will start to break down. At this point, a big shade suddenly covered a large area. Everyone looked up in amazement. The vimana of Atlanteans silently comes down from the sky. Hovering over the fortress, it begins to glow brightly, then a dazzling bolt strikes directly into the ram breaking the main instrument of assault in chips. A smell of burning wood fills the air. The crowd loudly screaming rushes in all directions. A few wounded are lying on the ground. Viman is gently lowered into the square, and three pilots in golden robes come out from it. The door opens, and the king of the guards comes to him. He invites them to the palace and orders his soldiers to take care of the wounded.

In the palace they are served with wine and food. The servants pour beverages and bring new dishes. Pharaoh said to his guests: 'Iltar and Votan, you've arrived just in time and helped us. Therefore we thank you. Nevertheless henceforth do not touch my people without my permission.

Iltar response to the king,

'Lord Arar-rat, you have accepted us as brothers. That's why we are grateful to you and to all your people. And we are happy to assist you in times of need. And I swear we wish your subjects only good. You, Aryans, are truly noble, because take care of your people even when you are in danger yourselves. Let your gods and the Low of One you always abide to save you!'

This improvised but quite a sincere toast caused an approving roar among all present. Then come the doctors to report that the wounded on the square are helped. Arar-rat lets all those who can walk themselves to their houses, and those who are still weak, may remain in the palace as long as they need.

The king says the Atlanteans of his peasants who were abducted and taken on Poseidonis. The guests express their readiness to assist in tracing and returning them. With the help of the magic mirror Atlanteans communicate with the advisor of the emperor in Alta. They tell him about the incident on the banks of the Nile. Adviser says that the authorities of Poseidonis are ready to find the kidnapped, if it be known who they are. They suggest to bring to them someone who knows the abducted or at least to look in the magic mirror in the presence of him. But after the last events it is impossible to call to the palace anyone of the blacks. It will take some time to make up for the experience of today's events. Pharaoh decides to embark on a search later. Iltar and Votan bid farewell to the king, get back in their vimana and fly away from the plaza.

10. The Ireland. Retreat

It was well after midnight when someone loudly and commandingly knocked the doors of the house where Kukhulin slept. The young man immediately jumped up, grabbed the sword and opened the door. The messenger was the leader of the fortress. Right at the doorstep the messenger spoke and called him a name that was given to Kukhulin at birth and was barely remembered:

'Get ready quickly, valiant prince Setanta! Druid Myrddin has arrived, he brought an order from your father Sualtama Mak Rot to urgently leave the castle and return to the capital Emain Makha!'

'Why? What did Myrddin say?'

'Myrddin said that the senior druid Cathbad, the father of your mother Dehtire, saw with his eye of wisdom that Ekoss would be destroyed before dawn by the fomorians. And we all can be saved only if we all leave the fort immediately!'

'This means their vimanas from Aztlan have already arrived, and they will shoot the "Eye of Balor" at us! But if we do not stop them, they will destroy the whole of Olster!'

'I was ordered to escort you urgently to the commander!'

Together with the messenger Kukhulin rushes to the leader. In the light of the full moon they see flying birds that fly very low. As if feeling peoples' anxiety, they somehow did not fall asleep tonight. In a rapid and silent flow people move on the streets in the direction of the north gate.

Seeing druid, Kukhulin said to him:
'Glory to you, wise Myrddin! But when we step back, will the people of Aztlan not pursue us and seize our land?'

'Praise to you, too, fearless Setanta! Truly, these fomorians will follow us further. But it will be then, and now we must not delay, because they'll be here before dawn. We must lead our people out and save them.'

'I have to stop them, I have the Wings of the Wind!'

'You will not be able to get them above the city, the prince. They will see you. You can fight with them only over the rocks surrounding our fortress of Dundilgan. We are all going there now. I'll tell you when the time will come and you will be able to select the direction of the wind.'

They all straddle their horses and gallop after the soldiers who departed from the deserted fortress. The road climbs slowly into the mountains, and with each turn the escapees cast last looks at the abandoned Ekoss.

On the shore arrived Tuahell says met:
'I see that half of your soldiers have bandaged wounds. What kind of savage you met, Azeyotl?

'They threw molten metal and did not let my people approached the walls and open the gate. These barbarians do not fear death and fight like wild animals. While our Balamantu and others stay at home and wait for news from us, we have to fight. But with your Vimana we can suppress all their strength, Tuahell.

'You said right, we will not destroy own people unnecessary. I will rest a little while and then get into vimana before dawn. Soon they will see what is Mash-Mak!'

Azeyotl smiles contentedly and then invites his guest and his assistants in his tent to have dinner with them.

11. The Reprisal

The night is already ending. All the twelve thousand soldiers and their families who have left Ekoss, stop for a short halt at the high terrain. From there in the light of the sun they can see the valley lying at the bottom and even the narrow strip of the coast, where it does not hide behind a forest. Kukhulin and Myrddin together with the heads of abandoned fortress climb the nearest hill and look down. Very soon in the predawn darkness they see that there, where the sea is joined with the ground, a large white star, emitting rays in all directions, flashes brightly and raises in the sky. Then it moves a little bit, shifts in their direction and freezes. Breathless, the Celts are silently watching her. The star begins to blink slowly. Suddenly it releases a bright orange-red beam. The beam stays for some time, and the observers see their fortress in its light. They recognize walls and buildings familiar to many of them from childhood, but horrified and perplexed they see how the fortress seems to change its color. At first they do not understand what is happening. Then the stone walls and towers of the fortress begin to glow at first very dimly but then brighter and brighter until soon become similar to the color of molten metal. Along with such a terrible change their form and shape become also altered, losing the usual precision and angularity. The burning buildings soon resemble not a city, but rather wild hills and shapeless cliffs.

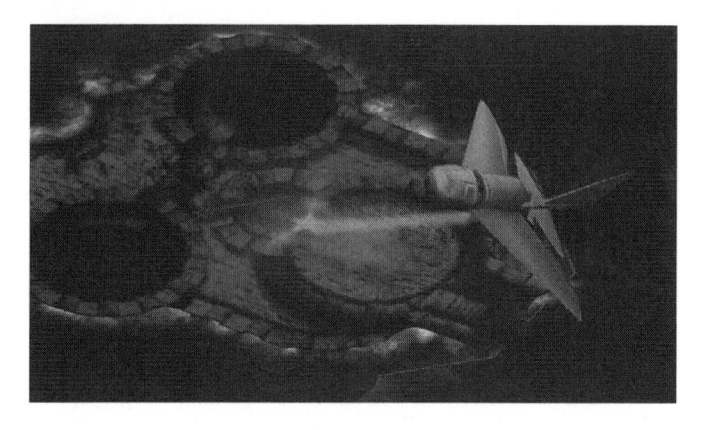

The brave leaders of the Celts stand dumbfounded until Kukhulin gives out a dull moan:

'Even the birds did not sleep, they also knew that the eye of Balor would be the last in your life ... Goodby, Ekoss...'

They are silent. Everyone who saw this, try to figure out, what they are facing and are aware that only the intervention of the wise Catbad and Myrddin saved them from the imminent death. The young soldiers have tears in their eyes, some of them left in their parents in Ekoss, who flatly refused to leave their hometown. Elders' wish is sacred, so no one could force them to go with them. Only a few young men remained with their old parents, and now all of them were burned alive and merged with stones. Morose, all the warriors of the Celts stand in twilight and gaze in the distance in the direction of their former fortress, already illuminated with the rays of sunrise.

Finally, one of the old generals asks a question, which springs rather from simple human wonder than from pain and depression:

'Kukhulin, what is the source of such a heat in the air chariot? After all, when the metal melts, stones continue to stay. To melt the stones you need an ocean of fire. Where do they get such power?'

'Father Conall, their entire force is transmitted through the air from the glass towers on their main island.'

'I've heard a lot about it, brave prince. But where do they get so much terrible power in the tower itself?'

'You see, it was built not by farmers and hunters, glorious Conall, but by the wise Magi. They made it of the whole mountain of rock crystal, which they found, freed from the earth and rocks, moved and raised to their home town and grind off all its countless facets. They have made the tower in such a way that it can collect all the sunlight in itself and transfer it to any place in the whole our world. Even at night, when there is only moon in the sky, the glass tower collects the reflected light of the sun from the moon. Now imagine, if they gather in one city or fortress all the light and heat of the sun that falls on the entire earth, then for sure even rocks will be scorched as from the volcano. We call it the eye of Balor, but they call this assembled power of the sun Mash-Mak. They told me that when their land was much bigger, those their ancestors who worshiped the gods of the night and its ancient king, the evil sorcerer Thevetatu, drove Mash-Mak inside the Earth to release its energy and join with theirs. In this way they wanted to become all-powerful, they wished to obtain the life full of pleasures and the ability of endless enjoinment unlike all other people. As a result the gods became angry, the underground fire intensified, volcanoes erupted and killed many of them, and the island has decreased greatly. Since then, they have become more cautious, and their ruler keeps the glass tower under protection and does not let anyone in. But vimanas can invoke the power of Mash-Mak at any place of the world. Glory to the goddess Morrigan and Danu, who via the sages warned everyone and saved us and our soldiers. And praise to you, the wise Myrddin! So far my blessed grandfather, I'll kiss him when we meet.'

Myrddin replies as if not to him but to those who are on the shore:

'The gods see everything, fearless Setanta! And they are always fair. Even if we won't be able to make fomorians pay for all this, the immortal themselves will force them to answer for what they did...'

'So be it, wise Myrddin! But you said that they will come to Dundilgan, and that I can fight with them there. When will they come?'

Myrddin closes his eyes and, after a pause, he says:
'Now they will place their people at the coastal valley, then their new ships will come, but it will be... in five springs ... Then only they will go to Dundilgan... '

PART 2

12. The Invasion

Little Horus grew gradually, and each year his hair would become a little darker. Blond and curly locks acquired more of a chestnut color. Quite early his parents noticed the boy's rare ability for learning and his excellent memory. It was enough for him to see any hieroglyph or hear any story only once, he could memorize everything and then accurately recall it with all the details. There was the only one book in their house. Before going into exile the old Ra-Ta left it specially for his future grandson. Asmini was already expecting a child, and her wise father, bidding her farewell, said she would have a boy, and when he grows up, they will see each other again. She did not tell Gorik the saddest details of those days, — let him learn about it when he grows up. Gorik every day learned new words and absorbed more and more in the grandfather's book, which told of the glorious deeds, majesty and wisdom of their ancestors. Every time when his father was visited by his friends officers, the boy was modestly silent in the presence of elders. But when anyone asked him about something related to history, he enthusiastically began to tell what he remembered by heart from the wise book and unspeakably surprised all the adults and even his parents, who every time admired him but not as their kid, but almost as an adult and a pundit.

Although Rame and Asmin always felt that he still loved them dearly, but at these moments he seemed to be someone else for them, almost a stranger, even though they experienced a surge of well-deserved pride. These evenings usually ended with the guests respectfully expressing their surprise for such an early maturity of thought of the child. They also used to reasonably conclude that the boy would be a worthy successor for them and the wise Ra-Ta, and unanimously advised to send him to the temple for learning. Rame taught his son martial art and would be happy if he followed in his footsteps. But he also took quite friendly any other choice of his son and often said that martial art is quite difficult and dangerous, and he would also prefer Horus to be taught by priests. When the boy was brought to the teachers, and when they saw his obvious intelligence and innate wisdom, having briefly discussed the matter, they have accepted him as a disciple and began to teach him. Since then when going to bed every night he couldn't wait to see the next morning, when after having only a cup of water he would go to school to learn and understand something new. Once, already nine years old Horus returned home after school, carrying scrolls of papyrus. After he took a meal of fruit which as usual was prepared for him in a large bowl, he noticed that his mother was sad and looked thoughtfully in the window. He came up to her, hugged her gently and, feeling her anxiety, said:

'Mom, why are you so sad? Something happened?'

Asmin caressed her son's head and sighed in response:
'War, my son...'

Black news reach quickly. No one knew for sure what was happening at the border, but total chaos began there. People of Chehennu, having left their familiar spots where they used to graze cattle, cultivate the land and hunt, with all their strength invaded the north-western provinces of the country and brought a complete devastation of everything that came their way. When Pharaoh learned that Hacho fortress was besieged in Lower Egypt, he could hardly wait for the next morning. He set out with two nearest divisions "Amen" and "Ra" to help his soldiers. The commander of battalion "Pta"and two others was ordered to urgently move in the same direction. Several times a day messengers raced on their horses from one marching division to the other to coordinate the movement of the whole army. And when after only three days Arar-rat stopped the troops an hour before sunset, he already knew that the division of "Pta" would be coming to the fortress by the night. Pharaoh gave his men a short rest, assembled his officers and only then he told them about the plan:

'Warriors of "Pta" will come to the Hacho before dawn. But the scouts of the enemy will be aware of them at night. Then in the morning they will have time to send there all their army, and many of our soldiers can die in the battle tomorrow. Therefore we will set out only in two hours. Let us go at night to get there by noon, and to our relief it will not be as hot as in the day.

The officers listened in silence, and only the chief commander said:

'Your decision is wise, Emperor! But I'm worried about one thing ...'

'What?', asked Pharaoh.

'Our soldiers, tired of the night march, will not bear a long battle.'

'True, my faithful Ani. But if we are late, then the enemy will gather more strength, and more my sons will fall in the fight. Therefore, we will rest in the afternoon, when we throw them back and get into the castle.'

Sanherib, the commander of "Pta" division, was already close to the target by the evening. He knew that the sovereign of Egypt with his army marches behind him in the night. He stopped for the halt after sunset, giving rest to his soldiers. With the dawn Sanherib saw Chehennu units that without keeping any formation in a large crowd like a stream flowed down from the nearby hills toward him. He moved his chariots and infantry forward. Egyptian commander knew that the enemy scouts saw his halt, and Chehennu were ready for battle. When the first ranks of soldiers with dark brown skin and white tattoos appeared on the way, Egyptians courageously attacked, but redeployed troops of Chehennu withstood the first blow and resisted, sometimes giving counterattacks. The whole area turned into a battlefield, the air was filled with the sounds of battle of the two armies: crashes from blows, war cries, whistling of arrows and darts, the tramp of horses' hooves and the roll of the chariots. The Egyptians were armed better, with their hopeshes that were made of a special bronze strong like iron. Their weapons looked more like battle-axes and pole axes than swords or sabers. They often dissected the shields of enemies, who had only short swords and long spears.

But groups of black soldiers continued to arrive in waves, flowing into ever-growing battle. It was still long before noon, a hot battle was unfolding around. Sanherib anxiously began to think that if his master does not arrive on time, very few of his warriors will remain alive. Chehennu withstood their attack and, with new and fresh forces, gradually began to press the Egyptians. To slightly reduce the front the commander of "Ptah" ordered to retreat slowly to the nearby woods and hills preventing the enemy from using the numerical superiority, which grew every hour. Squeezing the battle-line, Sanherib also reduced the risk of blows from flanks for himself and the encirclement of his division. The reserve was only a squadron of chariots, which was uncomfortable to fight in a close overcrowded combat. The commander recalled it from the front line and kept it to repel any unforeseen attacks. He was well aware that it was necessary to withstand, no matter how much time it would take. Finally, when he moved his last troops to fight, he heard the distant sound of trumpets, carried by the wind from the right side. The distant sound repeated, it grew, and within fifteen minutes showed the first ranks of the division "Amon," led into battle by the pharaoh in a golden helmet glittering in the sun. They came from the side where just recently the enemy approached. The infantry ran in tight formation with spears and hopeshes at the ready and with archers on the chariots from each side. Archers were shooting at the enemy. And as soon as the army of the king joined the battle, to the sounds of the pipes on the opposite side appeared the front ranks of the division "Ra", under the command of the chief commander of Ani. The ranks were not orderly but grew quickly. Chehennu obviously did not expect such a double blow. They wavered and began to retreat, but continued to courageously fight and did not turn their backs to the advancing Egyptians. The last, though tired from sleepless night march, feeling joy and enthusiasm and seeing that they came on time to help their troops, increased their onslaught until the enemy was completely thrown away and began to retreat disorderly. Having driven away the last and drastically depleted chains of enemies, the divisions of Arar-rat came to the fortress Hacho, where they met almost the entire garrison. The metal padded gate was wide open. It was cracked and had numerous dents from blows with the ram, but yet remained sufficiently strong. The soldiers threw up their hats and cheered, greeting his master:

'Lord Anahtu! Our lord Anahtu!'

Pharaoh stopped the horses, stepped down from the chariot and took the battle royal helmet off. At first the chief of the fortress came to him, bowed low before him, then proudly straighten himself and said loudly:

'Thank you, sir, you are our savior! Truly, o lord Anahtu, you are invincible, like your grandfather,

Araar-art the Great! Order your sons, Lord!'

The king wiped the sweat from his forehead and said softly in ensued silence:
'I order my sons to rest. We walked all night, and at the dawn our horses and foot soldiers ran to be on time to help Sanheribu. We heard the noise of battle from afar. And you, brave Horemheb, are praiseworthy for your loyalty — you did not surrender the fortress to the enemy and saved my army!'

'I am your humble servant, Sire! Live long, the ruler of Egypt!'

The chief of the fortress again bowed before the king and then showed him and the generals inside. Arar-rat ordered to deploy troops to rest. The fortress was not very big, and there was not enough space in a few rooms of the barracks. Tired soldiers in whole parties settled in the shades of walls and houses, in the towers of the fortress, and even on the streets.

But the commanders had no time to rest. They all gathered at the Pharaoh's to obtain an order from him what to do next. Soon, a group of the remaining officers arrived together with Ani, who said that the pursuit of the enemy stopped, all divisions are in the fortress, and those who did not find space in it, camped around it. At the end he added that among the prisoners there were Chehennu's leaders and he ordered to bring them in the room. The prisoners were brought; Pharaoh's tired face grew stern again. One of them was much taller than others; by his appearance he obviously stood out from the crowd. He was wounded in the right arm above the elbow, but his wounds were already bandaged by the Egyptian healers. The king flashed with his eyes, red-rimmed from sleepless night and long stress. He asked the black:

'Who are you and what's your name?'

The tall man replied with head held high, looking contemptuously right in the winner's eyes:

'I Teukalli, the eldest son of Massena, the main leader Chehennu!'

Pharaoh did not avert his eyes, and continued with a faint smile:

'And how many of our things looted the eldest son of the leader Chehennu?'

'I do not need someone else's property, Pharaoh, I am not a robber!'

'Then what were you doing in our area along with your people? Why did you come down on us like locusts? Why have you left your land and come here? Don't you know what fate awaits our enemies?'

Wounded prisoner again raised his head proudly:
'You Arar-rat is a brave warrior! But I'm not afraid of death.'

Then he lowered his eyes and said sadly:
'And our land ... it is no more ...'

'How is it?! What happened to it?'

'What will happen to the land if even a drop of rain does not fall in two months? It's all dried up and shriveled. Trees and grass dried, cattle died by herds. We've no channels, and the Nile is far, and it flows only in your land... Then came the fire. The fire tornado, like a wall, passed through our lands. Entire villages were burned in the fire, all who did not flee were killed. When spring comes and the wind will spread the ashes, then where our land was it would be a desert. When we understood this, my father took everyone who was still alive to the water side, to the Nile. But your warriors stood on our way, o king. And we did not beg them; we just went on, so that our children could live. And now you came with your army, and you want to chase us back. But we will not go back. Quick and easy death in the battle is better than a long and distressful one with children and elderly at the side. Our soldiers were never

The captives became silent, the pharaoh's face turned calm and sad. He thought briefly, then slowly and quietly said:

'You all go back to your tribe. And you also tell your father to come and talk to me tomorrow morning. Let him come not as an enemy, but as my guest. None of my soldiers will not stop you. But you never dare to lift your hands against my sons. Remember all this and tell your father. And now you all go.

The confused prisoners looked at each other, but no one moved. They seemed to be frozen in place out of unexpected generosity of the one who only an hour ago was their enemy and fought with them. Only when Anna ordered his guards to lead them through the positions of the Egyptians and told them to let the captives through the next day as well, looking surprised in the king's direction, they went to the door. Pharaoh it seemed did not look at the others at all and was absorbed in thoughts. He began to understand why these dark-skinned fought so bravely and even after a double blow from both flanks did not want to retreat. He already knew from the reports of the scouts that there were not more than half of all soldiers of Chehennu here. With the expert glance of strategist he looked at the situation and realized with horror that even when the other two of his divisions, "Osiris" and "Monte", come up, the forces will be roughly equal because the enemy will move up their remaining troops. But desperate courage those doomed people who have lost their homes would lead in any case to serious consequences for him. And even if he, thanks to the superiority of his tactics and weapons, was able to defeat the enemy, he would lose most of his troops in the best case, and very few of them would return home alive. Before leaving the capital he sent an order to all his remote troops to move to the center of the country and to the north. But to leave the boundaries of the kingdom without protection was also dangerous and fraught with many consequences. So it turned out that, sparing prisoners, he also spared his people.

Thinking about it, he increasingly began to understand with his intelligence that though so unexpected for him and all the others, his heart, trained by his great grandfather, made very wise and right decision. When he was still immature young men, Araar-aart the senior to the surprise of his generals let free his captivated and already defeated enemies at every opportunity, if they have not done anything vile and low. Answering to his surprised grandson's questions, old and wise warrior explained that a true warrior must be strong and courageous with a strong enemy, but toward the vanquished and defenseless he should be generous and merciful. He said that the enemy should fear and respect you, and then some day he will become your friend. And servant must genuinely love you to be your friend forever and not to become an enemy again. And he added that only a cowardly and wretched do the opposite — they fear of strong, but give vent of their anger at the weak with impunity. But it seems impunity only at first, because the gods are always fair. They will award each by right. Even the immortal gods, who can punish any proud mortal, always feel compassion and mercy at those whose eyes filled with sorrow and pain. King should try to be like gods themselves even in a very difficult situation. Then he will always have their protection and will be saved even when hope is already lost...

In the moments of such reflection Pharaoh distinctly felt the greatness and the infinite truth of the Law of the One. He knew how much depends on his word and will. If he commits a mistake, by succumbing to anger and folly, many of his soldiers, joyously standing now before him, will bleed to death on the battlefield. He is responsible for all of them to Heaven, and therefore he calls them his children. The king looked up and gazed thoughtfully at his generals and officers who, waiting for his orders, were talking quietly to each other. Rame from the division of "Amon" at the request of his colleagues showed them the lightning rod and explained how it worked. The king recalled that in the morning just before the clash of the two armies, when he was leading this division in the battle, a lightning twice hit the ranks of the enemy to the right of him. He asked the officer:

'Brave Rame, you shot with the lightning twice at the beginning of the battle. But then you fought with the usual sword. Why? Did the fire arrows run out?'

The officer stepped forward and honored the king by placing his right fist to his heart and bowing his head:

'Your Majesty, when the ranks closed, I was afraid to hit our own people. This fire weapon can only be used from a distance.'

'It is true, my son, I praise your prudence. And how did four of you — you, Razmik and his adjutants — manage to get rid of five people of Aztlan, whom all fear? After all, it was a moonless night. How did you fight without seeing them?'

'Verily thou, our ruler, know everything that happens to your people! It is true there was indeed no Moon that night, but we have not only eyes but ears as well. That's why myself and Razmik occasionally train our soldiers to fight with eyes closed. I always knew it would someday be required, but I never thought I would be fighting with Aztlan people. When they broke the gate of our house and entered the yard, we hurled darts at them and then advanced toward them using swords and khopeshes. Within a matter of two minutes they retreated, and when the dawn broke, we saw five bloody tracks from the wounds on the ground, and we realized that they were five.'

'Right you say Rame. My grandfather Araar-aart the Great taught me — all that you foresee will be your ally, and all that you don't will be your enemy. And today we have acquired victory, because we followed his teachings. Do you remember what he said about the interaction of forces?'

'I remember, o ruler of Anahtu! Araar-aart the Great taught that when all the parts and units are together and when they begin the battle exactly at the appointed hour, they can win at the small loss. And if they are too far from each other, then the more the other is late, the greater loss they will suffer. And the enemy will be able to defeat them separately.'

'Right, Rame. Truly, the gods are always fair, and

the fiery rod of Aztlan robbers went to a brave and dignified warrior of mine...'

There come messengers from the watch points and report to the king that the advance of units of the two far divisions "Osiris" and "Monte" have already appeared on the horizon. The king let all to rest and orders to call the officers who are going to their ranks in the fortress.

The next morning, the gray-haired Massena dressed as a chief priest along with his eldest son Teukalli and a small group of soldiers comes to the posts of the Egyptians, who, carrying out the order, let them all into a fortress. All Chehennus enter the hall where the king is having breakfast with his senior commanders. Pharaoh invites them to sit at the table and treats his former enemies. Hungry for many days, dark-skinned warriors eagerly pounce upon the food, but the chief and his son, despising hunger, eat slowly and calmly. After the meal, Pharaoh saw a deep sadness in the eyes of the old chief and asked him:
'Do your people abide the orders of Massena?'

'I can order them to die in the battle, o king, but I will not tell them to starve to death.'

'True, no father wants death for his sons. I can spare you, but only if you all fulfill my will.'

A pause. Then the leader asks:
'What will be your order?'

Pharaoh speaks slowly and calmly:
'You live. But never raise your hands upon the

children of mine, and none of them will touch you. You will have your villages parallel to the Nile Valley from Hermopolis to Abydos. Your people should work and dig channels. I will send my foremen, who will measure the land and water. You will pay tribute of tithe later, after you sow fields and collect the harvest. If an enemy comes in our country, all your soldiers will act with my army. If the enemy attacks you, I will send my men to defend your village. You, your son, and all your people should swear to never transgress my will and the will of my children. Choose!'

Massena responds after a pause:
'I am old, but I do know one thing — one should swear loyalty and to surrender only to a merciful master. When yesterday I was told that my son fell in battle, I realized that the gods are on your side, Pharaoh. And when you let him live and he came back with wounds bandaged by your healers, I realized that you are merciful. And since you care of others' children as of your own, it is true — the gods are fair by giving you victory. I will not go against their will. No more enmity between us and you, lord of Egypt. You are worthy to be the father of all of us, and we swear your allegiance. We will never violate your words, o generous sir. May gods protect you! Peace to your home.'

assena stands up and bows to the king; all Chehennus follow his example. Pharaoh responds and looks at the sun:
'Peace to our homes, because they are now truly united! Praise to you, Lord of Heaven, Amen.'

13. The heathen temple in Peose

The sun had already disappeared behind the sea, when guards allowed black slaves to return to their barracks to rest. No sooner slaves fell asleep tired of working in the hot-air of Poseidonis, than Tamil returned. The senior servant of the master used to normally send him once a week in the evening to the port with a cargo of fruit collected by the slaves. Every time after that the Egyptian used to tell a lot of interesting news. But this time he came back later than usual. Old Afteb asked his nephew:

'Well, what's the news, Tamil, was there anyone from our land?'

'Uncle Afteb, today as before I saw none of our fellows there. We got there late, the way after noon, because the new redskin slaves that work in the gardens, where we collected the fruit last spring, happened to be quite stupid. Perhaps, the old Zuluum caught them somewhere in the woods — they are complete savages: they can neither work, nor speak decently. They even hardly understand anything and only mooing angrily in response. Therefore the guards keep them in chains and whip them at each step. Thanks gods, we are all grown on the land and we accustomed to work since childhood. Therefore the master's men do not goad us in vain. They allow us to roam without the shackles, and it makes their life easier — they lead us to the field, show us the place and that's it; they can relax until sunset. And we do everything ourselves, we collect the harvest and carry it to the warehouse. But these new cannot work like this. They make the guards sweating along with themselves. The guards get angry and scold them, and whip them on the backs on the slightest pretext...

'That's right, a person without love for work is worse than an animal. Even domestic animals know how to work. And if people behave like wild beasts, then they will be treated like beasts. Is the city port too crowded with people and ships in the evening?'

'There are many of them wherever you turn your eyes, either in the morning or in the evening. Crowds of people carry cargoes. Ships raise above the houses and surround them on all sides as far as the eye can reach, and you can hear so many languages that it blows the mind...'

'What do they say?'

'I did not understand everything they were saying among themselves, but those who originate from here or from other cities of their island, it seems, again discussed mostly that it is time to assemble to soon move to other lands. They called various places and told each other, which was good and which was bad. But I did not understand many names and I could not ask them. But as I understood, some of their people have already moved off to the east, while others were preparing to follow them.

'And what is it that drives them from their native lands? Why can't they stay in one place? They had built such large and luxurious palaces so brightly bedecked with all kinds of different colors and many precious stones and metals. They have so much water, trees, flowers and birds around. Their land is so generous — you harvest crops in one field, and before you know it, it is time to collect crops from the second field. Will they abandon all these and go away? Don't they feel sorry for that, and why?

'I do not know. They said something about the underground fire, but I did not understand anything. Is there a fire under the ground?'

'So that's what it is! When the earth shook here, the old said that it was because of an underground fire, controlled by the gods ... And then they get angry at people...'

'Uncle Afteb, they called you this morning to the temple in the palace. You're probably able to see their gods. Tell me what they look like — similar to ours?'

'Yes, Tamil, there priests are being served by the oldest servants. I turned out, one of them fell ill today and therefore they called me. There was only one large and golden statue of god. The statue was beautiful. Three priests burned incense, chanted incantations and performed sacrifices in front of her. We were carrying vessels for them, but we put them on the floor and waited until they would call us to the altar before the statue. They called me only one time, so I went up to the statue. I looked at the gold statue and froze...'

'Why, Uncle Afteb, their God is so fearsome?'

'No, my boy... I was taken aback because the

statue had the face of our master...'

Then all the others, who were listening to his story in silence, rose from their seats and gathered around the old man. Affected by this story, his sons and grandsons, nephews and daughters asked in a discordant chorus:

'How is that? It means, our master is god, grandfather...?'

The old man was silent, not knowing what to say. Everyone, forgetting about sleep, was waiting for what he would say. And he finally spoke:

'I do not know, my dear. In his appearance he is just a rich man. I do not know what to think...'

'Father, maybe his ancestor was a god, and he just looks like him and therefore a statue is such?'

'Maybe so, my son... The only thing is that priests called the name of our master several times during their spells and they appealed to the carved image...'

'Maybe he took the name of his ancestor to be proud of it?'

'Yes, son, life is great and everything is possible in it. But here is what I think... What if he has become intoxicated out of his wealth, what if he got a false idea that he is god because his kinsmen worship him? After all, this could be... Only then, as I understand it, the real gods, who see and know everything, will unlikely be happy by this. And if they get angry, they can shake the whole earth, and send the underground fire at them. As all the priests unanimously repeat, for the great and all-powerful nothing is impossible. Since the people of Aztlan have become so terribly puffed up and lost their head and conscience because of their wealth, then the gods will certainly punish them. And then it turns out that what Tamil heard in the port about an underground fire was indeed true. It seems they all know this and already think where to move to save themselves and their loved ones. But where can you hide from the anger of the gods? You will not find such a place on whole earth to escape...'

14. The Decision

The news that the Pharaoh defeated the invading alien army, and then graciously allowed the vanquished to live on his land, quickly spread throughout the country. The leaders of the black tribes were concerned about this. They had a counsel, and the next morning they all came to the king. For the first time in many years after that memorable assault of the palace, when white-faced and black-skinned were split into two hostile camps, they appeared before the ruler of Egypt. Arar-rat remembered everything that happened then, but he did not like to stir the past, especially if this might lead not for the better, but for the worse. He was well aware that his people should live in peace and not be discriminated by color and faith in the gods, otherwise the lives of everyone will turn into one universal suffering, and then the Egypt simply disintegrate into many small territories inimical to each other. The leaders slightly bowed before the king, and the oldest of them said:

'Lord of Egypt, we have heard that you've allowed Chehennus live close to our villages. But their number is great. And where we go with our people?'

Arar-rat calmly replied:
'You need not to go anywhere. None of them will touch you. They swore to be always faithful to my will and never raise their hands upon my people.'

'But there are too many of them, and our land will not be able to feed everyone!'

'They will settle near the border and will not be part of your territory. They will build canals to the Nile. There will be enough water for all enough, we will measure and share it equally. Whole land of these unlucky people was dried up and the villages were burned. And since we, whitefaced, recognized them as our brothers and spared them, then you could take these black-faced as your brothers, if you listened to the voice of your heart.'

The words of Pharaoh have embarrassed the leaders a little, but the oldest did not agree with him and went on:
'You, Arar-rat, have accepted red-faced as brothers and let them into the country. Already many thousands of them came, they've built new villages and cities here, but do they recognize us as their brothers? They keep servants and call them living things and even do not consider them as people. And they maintain exactly the same attitude toward us, though we are not of their tribe and are not their servants! None of them made friends with us. If they

need something from us, they pay with their coins, and do not even ask our names!'

Pharaoh did not like many disputes from them was not good. And he was a man of action and make decisions quickly:

'It is all true, Mayum! But friendship and brotherhood are not caused by orders, but by the dictates of the heart. Every heart, than only one. *Therefore* it takes time. What can I do for all of you so that you stopped being afraid of people of Chehennu and Aztlan?'

These words made all present silent and thoughtful. Now they themselves realized that it was impossible to return five stolen years back without their participation. And that Arar-rat will not send the arrived nations back. Though Atlanteans look down on the locals, but behaved quite peacefully, and so there were no new kidnappings or crimes during this time. It turned out that Pharaoh was right, convincing everyone that they were his friends and that they shouldn't be feared of. So what then they should ask the king about? All were silent, and Mayum boldly looked straight in the king's eyes as if thinking, weather the king would agree or not. Finally the black leader firmly and quietly said:

'Return Ra-Ta!'

Now Pharaoh became thoughtful. Chief commander came to the throne:

'The lord must remember that nine years have passed since Ra-Ta was sent to Abyssinia, and that many noble and grand people and councilors demanded to expel him from the country?'

Mayum did not wait for the king's decision, so he told the commander:

'Because for the wise Ra-Ta all men were truly brothers. And when some of white people oppressed our men, he always defended the blacks. If you, sir, really want all people of your country to live as brothers, then you will return our wise friend. And you should not remember the lies that he was unjustly accused of by your advisers, who said he biased the blacks against the white-faced and wants to embroil the nations.'

'Yes, Mayum, split between us began when during your rebellion the priest urged me to take your side, and when the present and much stronger enmity began, he had been long in exile. Had he been here, he would have not allowed the new strife, because you listened to him more than me or any of white-faced. Ani, call Iltara to me!'

'Yes, my lord!'

'And tell me, Annie! Our Rame from the division of "Amon" is married to the daughter of a priest, isn't he?'

'Truly so, lord.'

'Then the call him to me. Mayum, you can tell people that Ra-Ta will be back soon.'

'Wise decision, my emperor. All of us will be

happy to see him, and let your heart also rejoice!

'I will rejoice, Mayum, only when peace and brotherhood will flourish in my land. This is the will of gods. Let wise Ra-Ta help us with this.'

15. Retribution

Myrddin remembered his promise to the prince. When it was time, all the Celtic army, led by the ruler Sualtamom Mak Rot, marched from the capital of Emain Mahi to the sea in the south. The wise druid Catbad walked near the king and ordered all the troops to maintain strict secret — they should move only at night and during the day they should hide in the woods and rocks. Kuhulinn and Myrddin were in the avant-garde.

On the third day at midnight the army came to the hills with Dundilgan fortress behind, which was already visible. Kuhulin Myrddin immediately started to reconnaissance. They peered into the darkness of night and under the moonlight they began to see what is happening on the ground. All units of the Celts had already been withdrawn from the fort a few days before the arrival of the troops of the King. They have located in the woods and ravines, and strictly followed the order of their master: move only in the dark and in complete silence. No one could find their location, even with the most watchful eye. For some reason the prince began to recall the pictures from his childhood: he stood in the palace on the beautifully painted plates, illuminated by bright light of torches and lamps, and peered into the darkness. He was still small and did not realize what so fascinated and drew him in the window, what unknown distances and events contains the unknown darkness. But even then, he felt and clearly saw that danger and its concomitant anxiety makes his brave heart beating harder. And this state, as if familiar and welcomed, filled and surprisingly pleased and intoxicated him. He felt as if he had wings and he wanted to fly towards his future feats...

And now Kuhulin felt all this and realized that far back in his childhood his eye of wisdom had foreseen the future.

Meanwhile, something was happening in the plain. Lights were flickering, the wind brought snatches of distant sounds, and it was obvious that their enemies were clearly not sleeping and were getting ready for battle. The prince took off his shoes and began to spread the Wings of the Wind. Two long shafts, fastened with the top ends, parted to the sides. The firm leather, attached to the shafts by edge, straightened. The crossbar was installed in the middle, and this simple device started to really remind the wings of a large prehistoric bird. Myrddin was intently silent, his eyes closed. He was calling the lord of winds for help asking him to direct the prince to the goal. The wind intensified and blew straight in their backs. Kuhulin was ready. He tied himself to the bar with a belt and, so as not to start ahead of time, he clung tightly to the ledge of a rock with his bare feet. Tension grew by each minute, and then, finally, a white large star flared brightly far below and, beaming all around, rose to the sky — it soared the vimana of Tuahella as it was then, in Ekoss. Myrddin said excitedly: 'It's time, brother Setanta! You alone will lead the battle in the sky, so let gods help you!'

Kuhulin pulled away from the ledge, ran a few steps to the edge of a cliff and, pushing off strongly, took off. A powerful jet of wind quickly carried him forward and up. The star, floating in the night sky, was quickly approaching. He already began to distinguish the reflection of the device in the dark and has sent his vehicle toward the tail of the vimana.

When he reached directly above it, the prince made a smooth circle and quickly landed on its tail. Having caught the body of the vimana with his bare feet, he sat down and unbuckled a long iron axe from his belt. Two metal cylinders gleamed directly in front of him in the moonlight, each had the size of a large millstone. He knew that the force driving vimana is in them. He also remembered that all the parts of the vimana are made of lightweight metal which was a bit softer than iron. People from other lands hardly ever heard about it. The entire calculation and all hope of a brave Celt were based on this. But, as five years ago in Ekosse, time was short. Vimana slowly began to flicker. This meant only one thing and it was the worst thing: the enemy is gathering strength for the fire attack on the fortress, and soon the vimana turn it into only melted rocks and hills. Kuhulin came close to metal cylinders, and, feeling a thin slit in the junction, where they were attached to the body, he began to push the edge of an axe blade in it. The material was not as strong as the red-hot iron of Celtic weapons, and under the pressure of Prince it began to succumb. He managed to move apart the edges of the joint and with his fist he energetically stroke on the back side of his battle-ax. He was able to squeeze it in half a finger. Then, gripping the shaft at both ends and twisting it, he began to separate the cylinder from the edge of the main body. Finally, he was able to tear off the first cylinder. He threw it down and immediately took up with the second one. But having lost one of its engines, the vimana rocked and began to descend like a falling leaf. Kuhulin furiously tore off the second engine, ignoring the fact that he was getting closer to the ground. When he managed to tear off, the plane began to fall rapidly, but the prince pushed off and soared up again into the air, he flew a couple of hundred steps, and before he touched the ground, he heard as if a flying chariot collapsed on the ground behind with a clatter of falling armor.

Kuhulin unfastened himself from the crossbar of the Wings of the Wind and heard the sound of an opening door of the defeated vimana. Pilots poured out from it, swaying and falling to the ground. Kuhulin was not sure whether they were those who five years ago destroyed Ekosse; that time he saw their unit only from afar as a point of light in the darkness. But he still felt such a hatred, which he had never experienced before to anyone. Forgetting about his Wings already blown by the wind, he ran to them. On the go he unleashed a pair of short special darts on his back, and, as soon as his eyes spotted the figures of enemies, he immediately threw the first dart at them, hitting one of them on the shoulder. Atlanta screamed, but then he pull a bloody dart out of the wound, turned around, and having spotted the Celt, he threw the weapon at him. Kuhulin dodged and run up closer. At a distance of ten steps he threw a dart at another, hitting him in the chest. Atlanta dropped his weapon and just like the first, he pulled out the dart from the wound. But he had no time to throw it back. Kuhulin gave his opponent such a strong blow on the head with his axe that the helmet cracked, and Atlanta fell dead to the ground. But after a moment, the one he had wounded the first, bleeding, rushed at him. Celt grasped Kuhulin with both hands and squeezed so powerfully that Kuhulin's bones cracked, and his eyes darkened. But he quickly regained his ardent spirit. Although he could not even take a breath, squeezed in the powerful arms, he was not going to give up or lose. Because the axe in his hand was squeezed between him and the enemy, the prince took this opportunity and made a sharp push with all of his squeezed body. While falling with the wounded enemy, at the moment of impact with the ground he was able to drive his axe with all the strength under the enemy's chest. Atlanta faintly screamed and pried his deadly embrace. When Kuhulin got up, he saw a third driver. Tuahell stood between deformed doors of the crashed vimana and aimed his weapon at the Celt. Prince noticed the red light on the Atlanta's staff and realized that now it would strike with the lightning. Knowing that he had no time even to evade the blow, he instantly threw the axe from the lower position, hitting the pilot in the arm at the very moment when he shot. The staff flew out of the pilot's hands, and the lightning already released struck in the air. Seeing that the enemy is also now unarmed, Tuahell ran to him and grabbing him by the throat with both hands, began to strangle him. He hold the enemy's throat with a grip of steel. In spite of sharp movements of the prince Tuahell was not going to let him go. Kuhulin estimated the strength of the Atlant's hands, but kept trying to break away from him. Because of his abrupt jolts they only slightly changed their place of battle, but Kuhulin could not break away and began to feel that he was losing consciousness. Having made another and a last desperate effort, he again was not able to escape. But he moved back a few feet away and felt with his foot a shaft of his javelin on the ground. Thanking the gods for their help in the battle, Kuhulin with a speed of a lightning grabbed the dart with his big and second toes and gave his foe a master stroke in the groin. But this time instead of a spear Celtic hero used a short dart that was exactly fit for the close range combat with the Atlants or Fomorians, as they were called by other Celts. Tuahell screamed and at once benumbed out of pain and loosened his grip. The prince was finally able to pull away, but then again he felt the most overwhelming hatred that drove him to fight before. Unable to resist it, he rushed to vimana, picked up his axe and ran back to the frozen Tuahellu. Kuhulin made a jump on the move and reaching the enemy, he cut his head off in one stroke. And only then he felt that his smothering hatred began to subside. When he composed himself a little after such a severe unequal battle, the prince began to discern people who were running to him in the darkness with torches and called his name. It was Myrddi who first came out of the darkness. Seeing Kuhulin in the light of torches, standing alone next to the viman and three defeated enemies, who each was a head taller than him, the Celts bowed to the prince as a token of profound reverence.

Then Myrddin broke the silence by saying that the enemies were coming there soon and it was time to leave. Kuhulin did not argue with his wise friend, and together they went back into the darkness to tell all the soldiers and to the king of the new feat of prince...

16. Return

Horuse has already returned from the temple and was absorbed in reading a new scroll that his teacher gave him. Asmini was finishing cooking dinner for the arrival of her husband, who was called by Pharaoh. Glancing briefly in the window, she suddenly froze for a moment, and then, surprised, she said:

'Son, what is that?'

Horuse left the book and came up to the window.

In the sky floated a large bird, sparkling in the sun. Approaching their home, it started to land. Horus and Asmin went out into the yard, Razmik and his squire were already there. The officer was holding a sword and commanded to bring the darts. He said it vimana of Aztlan, but what is he doing here in the afternoon? Maybe these are the robbers returned to avenge for their old defeat? While they watched, puzzled, all the passers-by on the street scattered around, and viman slowly sat down on the ground. It was only when people in the golden dress came out of it along with Rame, who, slowly talking to pilots, invited them into the house, the alarm went away, but their surprise increased even more. Razmik went to meet the guests and said with a smile:

'Brother Rame, do you already serve in the army of Aztlan?'

'Brother Razmik, we all serve our master and the One. Let me introduce you to our red-faced brothers Iltar and Wotan. They are valiant warriors. It is they who could help us out when black-faced wanted to seize the palace of Pharaoh.'

While the men acquainted to each other, and the guests expressed their respect to the Aryans for punishing thieves from their island, Asmin and Horus approached them and stood modestly silent, listening to their conversation. Rame again invited all to come in the house, then he went to his wife and said:
'My beautiful wife prepared a lavish meal, because we brought her a great joy. Sister Asmin, feed all the mighty warriors before a long journey!'

'Before the journey, Rame? Did Pharaoh order you to hit the road?'

'We're all going on a journey, dear. The lord Ararrat ordered to return Ra-Ta! With the help of Iltar and Wotan we will see my wise father-in-law today before sunset.'

The woman's eyes flashed to tears:
'I saw him in a dream today, he told me, "Horuse has grown, my daughter." So that's what it meant...

Horuse, who was standing at the side, could not hold himself:
'Dad, I'm coming with you, too!'
'Yes, my son, today you will finally see your grandfather!'

The boy jumped out of joy and was about to kiss his parents, but, remembering that they were hosting guests, he composed himself.

The lunch was quick, all were accustomed to marching conditions. They heartily praised the owner, who happily fussed around the table and totally forgot about eating. Then they said goodbye to Razmik, got into viman and took off. Iltar asked Asmin to put her right hand on the console and then remember and keep in mind the face of her father, so that sophisticated navigation instruments of their vehicle could find him in space and hold to the course. Asmin said she didn't need to remember it is not necessary, because the face of her father was standing in front of her eyes from the very morning. Surprised

Horus was examining the ground from the window; he had never seen houses so small. Fascinated, he watched how sunrays reflected in the waves of the river.

People were so tiny that they seemed like ants. The landscape at the bottom changed all the time. Only an hour later he already saw the rapids of the Nile that his teacher used to tell him about. Then mountains became higher and higher, and below he could see the temples carved in the gray rocks. Finally, another hour passed, the river completely disappeared from view, the winged car slightly changed its direction and began to decline. At the bottom he saw a large garden at the edge of which stood a house. Dark-skinned people sat in front of him in two long circles. They all held scrolls and listened to an old man dressed in white. When they saw the vimana coming down from the sky, they all stood up, and the old man without the slightest fear first came to the aircraft. Two soldiers with spears separated from the crowd, followed him and then stood behind him.

When Iltar opened the metal door, Asmin first jumped onto the grass and ran to the old man. The poor woman was in tears of joy, she haltingly told him everything that had happened today. Briefly she mentioned some of the important events that took place during his long absence. He hugged her and stroked her head. All were silent, observing the meeting of the daughter and the father. The more Horus looked at his grandfather, the more he was surprised that his grandpa looked exactly as he always imagined. Even his glance seemed to him as native and close as the glance of his father or mother. Asmin coped with her excitement and just smiled happily. Rame kissed the hand of an old man, who, in response kissed him fatherly in the forehead and then came up to Horuse. Only now Horus saw how shiny his eyes were. It was not like the usual smile, although Ra-Ta was smiling slightly. But Horus never saw such light that streamed from his eyes in anyone. The boy realized to his surprise that though he was extremely happy to at last see his grandfather, he experienced even greater joy from this kind and gentle light that went straight into his heart, the glance that saw all his thoughts and dreams and at the same time did not seem to be sharp or piercing. Imitating his father, Horus kissed the hand of an old man, then straightened up and unexpectedly even to himself said:

'What a wonderful light in your eyes, grandpa!'

Old Ra-Ta grinned and kissed his grandson on the cheek and said,

'Yes, you are already wise, my dear boy. May gods protect you.'

A group of black men with scrolls came closer and surrounded him the all sides. One of the approached asked the priest:

'Master, are you leaving us?'

Ra-Ta appealed to all:

'Pharaoh is calling me back. But those of you who want to study further and are ready to break away from their homes can come with me to Egypt.'

The students were taken aback a little bit; they clearly were not prepared for such sudden and serious decisions. Only two young men said they wanted to follow the priest. They went home to obtain the consent of their parents to this journey for knowledge. The rest humbly thanked the priest for everything he has taught them over the years, and departed. The guards, who were also the Egyptians sent by Pharaoh to guard the priest-in-exile, rejoiced even more than himself. That time they were still young, so over the years they have grown up and, of course, missed their native land. Ra-Ta invited everyone in the house, he served them local fruit and then began to pack for the road. His load was small: mostly books in different languages. He asked about certain people and events, Asmin and Rame answered and Iltar and Wotan listened to their conversation in silence.

Horus was shifting his gaze from his grandfather to his mother's happy face and back and thought how suddenly comes true what you want the most and what you wait for so long. By the evening, two young men came back, they were very happy; their parents agreed for their studies in Egypt. Their inspiration doubled because now, finally, with their own eyes they would be able to see everything they had heard about this great country, as well as to continue to learn from their wise teacher, who they loved almost as much as Horus. Ra-Ta was soon ready. He warmly said goodbye to the master of the house, then they all sat together in the viman and, taking off in the darkening sky at sunset, took the road to home.

On the way back, Horus, looking out the window at the burning stars, listened with amazement how his grandfather talked with the pilots. Ra-Ta asked about the cities of Poseidonis, about the temples of the gods, about the ancient doctrines and the law of the One. He was eager to know so many different things. He asked about the people who lived on the island, about their places and customs. Priest unmistakably called the names of many nations, he even knew what shade of color each of them had. His words were so clear and confident that others asked him how many times he visited their island:

He said: 'Not even once in this earthly body, but many times in my past lives. However, soon I'll have to go to your great country, because the case in Egypt requires this.'

The pilots looked at each other in surprise, it was evident that they appreciated the character of the old man, because even on their island rarely did they see such deep knowledge. Then Ra-Ta said to Atlanteans: 'What kind of alloy your vimana is made of?'

Iltar said: 'It is the alloy of three metals, two white

and one red.'

'I believe the red is copper? Or is it your famous sparkling orichalcum? What are the two white ones?'

'That's right, Ra-Ta. The main metal, constituting more than eight-tenths of the alloy, is produced on our island in the most hot and humid places. We called it the king of metal, as in the ground it is much more than all the others. Its ore looks like an ordinary clay, although we do not take ordinary clay for it but choose the one which is fit for it. Then our master metallurgists add special white minerals to it and release Mash-Mak in this mixture. It becomes very light silvery metal, it is the lightest, but it is not known in other lands because they cannot get it from any ordinary ore like other metals. And the power of Mash-Mac is unknown to them, too. That is why there is not even a name for this metal in your language. The same is with the second one. We extract it directly from the sea water. It is as silvery-white. And if you bring fire close to it, it can burn brightly even in the open air.'

Rame asked in surprise: 'How can you get the metal out of the water? You are truly magicians!'

'Not out of the water itself, but out of salt of the seawater. However, both of these metals, and especially the first, are very soft, but when combined with copper their alloy, if you leave it for a few days in the heat, becomes much stronger and firmer. Usually we add not more than one-tenth of copper, and not more than half of the one tenth part of the second metal.'

The next question asked Ra-Ta: 'Well, with this ratio the color of the alloy should be almost white, not gold?'

'Right, but our masters apply a layer of a special substance on the surface to preserve the alloy from destructive effect of air. That's why we can choose any color of the coating. There are many golden colors, but there are also blue and turquoise, which equally shine under the sun and even in the dark.'

Then they began to discuss the energy used in the aircraft.
'What kind of power does your vimana use in flight?'

'Force of attraction and repulsion', the pilot replied shortly.

The elder understood everything at once as if he did it all his life:
'In the earthly world opposites are attracted to each other, therefore all living entities walk on the earth and, besides birds and flying insects, they rarely break away from it. So you change the state of the vimana's body, making it similar to the terrestrial attraction, therefore the earth pushes the vimana away. I heard that your machines receive all their power from a power crystal, huge like a mountain. The crystal is located on your island and collects the sunrays. But how is this power transmitted to you in the air?'

In response Iltar invites him in the tail section.

There are large rectangular containers made of pure gold. The pilot opens the lids and shows leather bags inside. He unties one of them and shows its content to the Egyptian. He seems not very surprised and thoughtfully says:
'Excellent grain, large and clean. Wheat loves the sun and collects its strength even under the ground, when sunrays do not fall on it. But it will not sustain intense heat of the sun and can then just burn like from fire?'

'Truly, you are wise, Ra-Ta, because you rightly judge even about what you see for the first time. Grain just helps the rays to find our ships in space. Then the current of power flows through the metal and crystals.'

'Mash-Mak? You Atlanteans thus call the ether of gods. We Egyptians call it Eter, as well as our great river, because there is also a heavenly river apart from the earthly one. Our ancestors also called the ether by the name Ra, which is the name of the sun god, because all of us are his children and our life force we get from him. The gods do not care how we call the ether; the main thing is we should not use its power for evil.'

'Truth thy mouth hath spoken, Father. We must always remember the law of the One.'

'Right you say, my son. The wound in the hand of the other hurts the same as in your own. And all what we do for others will returns to us, so that we understand that we do it only for ourselves, for truly we are all One.'

17. The Council

No sooner Mayum learned that Ra-Ta returned home than a messenger arrived and called him to the Council of Pharaoh. Mayum realized that his old friend would be there, too, so, he hurried. He was not mistaken: Ra-Ta sat silently with a group of senior priests of the Aryans and together they all listened to the chief priest of the blacks. Priests and Hierophants of Aztlan sat in a separate group and there was a woman among them. To his surprise Mayum noticed that among the Hierophants of the Aryans there was also a woman. When he looked harder, he recognized the great priestess of Isis, who almost never left her room on the eighth floor of the main temple of the Goddess. Even the stairway that led to her was covered with leopard skins so that nobody's steps prevented the priestess from hearing the voice of the Lady if she would say something that should be immediately conveyed as the order for the chief Hierophant and Pharaoh. Mayum also heard about the wisdom of the red-faced priestess from Aztlan. He knew that her name was Ree, and that she was highly honored by her people. The meeting was certainly very important, but Mayum had no idea how Arar-rat would be able to resolve all conflicts between the nations of the country even with the help of his old and wise friend, who only two days ago returned from his exile. The black population of Egypt seriously feared that Arians could accept the faith of the arrived islanders and then they would end up in the minority. Because of this their own faith would no longer be honored and could severely be shaken. The high priest of the blacks spoke strongly but with a hint of bitterness in his voice; he criticized the white-faced, who, as considered his men, betrayed their friendship with his people and who were ready to worship the gods of the strangers:

'As I heard, your people now go more in Aztlan temples than in their own. They want to know the laws and customs of others, and your priests quietly allow it. In this way you will stop to honor not only our gods, but tomorrow you will forget your own. We will then have to part with you all and to live by our own laws with our gods and our troops! It is nearly already seven centuries since red-faced built their pyramids next to the great Sphinx. But for every one hundred years hardly one or two of our black priests received initiation there. If they did, it was only the very first and small, though they take as many of your students as their own. They treat us just like their slaves, whom they calle living things! They believe we are undeveloped savages, but you make friends with them and so you are at one with them! The people of our brothers, Zulus, have already left their homes and moved far to the south searching for new places. And we can only follow their example. But we do not want to leave the land of their ancestors. And while leaders think what to do, our people are now trying to avoid even the unnecessary talk with you...

The priest paused and sat sadly in his chair. All were silent. The main Hierophant of Aryans spoke first: 'Brother Tehena, true Aryans are always ready to learn from anyone who has wisdom. Neither I nor our king do not find anything wrong in it. Sadness does not allow you to judge wisely. Why do you think that they will forget about our gods? And let me remind you that even the greatest of the gods, as well as the people and all living beings are but parts of the One Creator...

The black-skinned priest replied: 'Hept-Saft, no matter how much you speak about the One, let me remind you that our master Seth did not accept the teaching of Osiris, for Osiris also came from foreign lands!'

'We remember this, Tehena, for Osiris came from the East long before Arart the Great and he was also Arian. But remember that when Seth's servants killed the lord of the Kingdom of the Dead, it was Isis, who took the teachings of Osiris and gave his wisdom to the people. Remember that Isis was born here in the Nile Valley. And when people stopped to quarrel over different interpretations of the words of the gods, which actually express only the will of the One, the peace came to the country and Egypt began to prosper. Black, red and white people worked and fought together as brothers, though each of them worshiped their gods. What has changed now? Even if the number of red-faced increased do we all need to quarrel and separate from each other?'

Tehena said bitterly: 'The most important thing has changed, Hept-Saft. If this continues, then even our people will stop to honor their own gods, who are ignored by the newcomers. And then they will cease to obey their own leaders and kings. Uncontrollable people are more terrible than the invasion of the sea. Who can return it back to its shores?'

There was a silence. Everyone understood that divided nations should somehow return peace among each other until something even worse happen. But on the other hand, everyone was aware of how difficult it was to intervene in the affairs of the gods, when even the people could not agree among themselves. They spoke of the One but it did not help: there must be some action. But how could they act with such disbelief and not to cause a new enmity. Who could find such a difficult solution? And the old Mayum was not mistaken, this was the Ra-Ta:

'The water from the Nile is the same either for blacks, who call it "maat", or for Arians, who call it "uadzhur", or for red-faced, who call it "atl". No matter for the water how you call it, but for us water is essential, we cannot live without it. People of Araar-aart call even the great river by the name Eteru, the Grace of the gods. People of Tehena called it Ium, and your people, Mayum, call it Hapi...

Ra-Ta looked at his old friend and he happily recognized his calm and friendly glance of a person, who will never deceive and betray and who is always on your side. It was as if they had just parted yesterday, as if they weren't separated for many years, although both of them turned more gray. Ra-Ta continued and everyone listened attentively:

'But the great river gives its water to all and never asks who calls it how. Also the gods, even though they have different names, they all belong to the One and understand every speech. And they accept all the words told in love and reverence. The same your lord Seth is called Ash by western nations. To the east of Egypt he is revered as Hemti, but you know that he responds to all these names. He is one under all the names. Also all the gods having different names express different parts of the One. All the power and greatness of the heavenly beings is that they merged with the One and that they reveal His will. If we want people of different skin color to live on Earth in harmony and honor the gods of each other, we must help them to see that all the gods also make friends in heaven, for they are all in the One.

Pharaoh asked in surprise: 'We all recognize the One, but how to help people to see it?'

'And where do people see the faces of the gods? Sometimes the immortal do reveal themselves to the most deserving even in our ordinary life, but even a small child can always see their images in the temples'.

'Of course, everyone worships the gods in temples, but what do you mean?'

'Let new temples be built along with the old temples. In these new temples the gods of all the nations will be displayed together. And then even a child will understand that if our immortal gods, worshiped by all — black, white and red people — are friendly in the sky as members of one great family, then we on Earth should remain in peace, for we are all brothers. And nobody will be neglected, either in heaven or on earth. This is the only way to quickly appeal to the heart through the eyes of a man. You decide, sire!'

There was a silence. This advice was simple but its

uncommonness was striking, because before each god was worshiped in a separate temple. How will gods take it themselves? Would this bold innovation not cause their anger? Pharaoh asked the Chief Hierophant: 'What will the holy Hept-Saft say?'

'When the life is peaceful on earth, then the service to the gods takes place lawfully, but when the atmosphere is surcharged with hostility and desolation, the worship of them is neglected. Let black people be sure that their gods are being worshiped equally with the others. Wisely said our brother Ra-Ta. May it be so.

Although factions between people bring worries to the gods, still let the immortal themselves decide this important question — how to worship them. What will be their will?'

Everyone held their breath and waited for a response. In the deep silence the voice of the priestess Isis sounded softly:
'Ra-Ta told the truth. The will of the Mistress is with you. Decide, o king!'

Then there was similarly quiet voice of the priestess Ri: 'The words true of the elder and of our sister are true. Decide, sire!'

Then the king said:
'What will the sages of black people say?'

Here again there was silence. The priests and the leaders of the blacks looked at each other, but remained silent. Then stood Mayum and looking at his old friend's eyes uttered:

'True, Ra-Ta sees the heart of the One. Let people in the world be united like the gods in the sky. Praise to you, heavenly patrons, our friend found a wise decision...'

Pharaoh silently rose from his throne. Still being in deep thought of what he heard, he said:

'So be it... The solution is found, my brothers. Praise to the One... Thank you, wise Ra-Ta, you came back to our land on time. Amen...'

'Amen' — chorused the members of the council and, giving a nod to the king, began to disperse.

PART 3

18. The First Initiation

Gates closed behind and he found himself in total darkness. Only a thin strip of light ran across the floor and led to the depth of a corridor. Horus took a deep breath and moved forward. He remembered what he was told just before: 'You have to go fast without stopping.'

'Well,' he thought. 'If the whole point of the test is to go fast and not stop, then I will not stop.'

Horus walked as fast as he could, especially because it seemed to him that the corridor was not very large. At the other end of it he saw a bright light and it seemed to him that he would soon come. But as he approached the light, he began to notice some strange things — the gap was increasing, and it turned out that it was not the door aperture, but something very obscure. When he came closer, he began to distinguish something like a fire. Approaching more and more, Horus was convinced that it was indeed a strange fire. Someone in the underground corridor built a fire.

'How strange,' Horus thought. What should he do now? If he stops, then he will violates the conditions he had been told. He was told: 'Go quickly and do not stop.' If he doesn't stop, he can then be burned or his cloth may catch fire. Horus pondered what he should do, and still he kept on moving with the same pace. The fire, which was obviously burned before him, was growing, but it did not stop the young man.

He decided: 'Be as it may. If our teachers, who are so kind and so wise, told the student that he should not stop, it did not mean that he was sent to die and that he shall certainly die.' So many people passed this way before him. If it was so bad as it might seem, it means they all must have been burned to death? But the teachers themselves went through all that when they were still students. He was told that all must pass through all stages of testing. Even a son of a king or a chief priest could not avoid them. They all should have passed this test, and all of them are healthy and alive. Neither of them is seem to display any traces of burns — neither old nor young. So, there is nothing to worry about.

With these thoughts Horus kept going at the same pace. And when the fire was already in front of him, then only he noticed a strange thing: the fire had no heat. No heat and no sound. It was a quiet and mysterious flame, as if illusory. He has passed a few remaining meters and entered in the range of the fire. He felt the same thing: that was no heat. Nothing was burning on himself, no smoke, nothing made him choke. And so he continued to go ahead quietly, nothing prevented him to do so.

When he came out of the field of fire, he looked back once to make sure that all this was really taking place, and saw that the fire really burned in the back but it did not touch him. 'It is strange,' Horus thought. 'What could it be?' A result of some magic spells? Or his faith made such miracles? But he was not at all inclined to consider himself a master of magic, able to stop the fire.

Thinking thus to himself and not giving much importance to his thoughts, Horus continued to keep the same pace. After another five minutes the luminous streak led him to the end of the corridor. The corridor was over. He saw a door in front. He knocked. A few moments later the door opened. There stood his teacher and all his restrained appearance expressed goodwill and triumph. Only his eyes were smiling. Master said to Horus:
'Well, my son, you've passed the first test. It was a trial by fire.'

The teacher led him into another room with the images of different hieroglyphs on the walls and began to explain to him not only the meaning of each sign that Horus knew from childhood, but he went on to explain the value of the secret symbolism of each character on the wall. He said that only the one who knows the meaning of these signs can read ancient books and understand their words. 46

Horus was very interested, it was amazing. Although he was still very young, but those things that he used to consider familiar and understandable, had completely different dimensions and a much greater depth of which he may be suspected, but still could not understand and see it so clearly. This new and exciting experience lasted almost until sunset.

In the evening, when he was released, he returned back home, cheerful and happy. Parents were glad to see him, and his grandfather again paternally kissed him in the forehead and smiled. Horus could not resist. He decided to ask his grandfather about what he did not dare to ask teachers.

'Grandpa, why is in the cave a fire that does not burn?'

Old Ra-Ta smiled even wider. 'So, you passed the test, my boy?'

'Yes. I was told to go without stopping, and I did not stop, and nothing happened to me.'

'Were you not afraid that the fire would burn you?' asked the grandfather.

Horus said: 'I had no time to be frightened. I was told to go and not to slow down the steps. When I saw the fire I thought that all our teachers, too, passed this test. If they escaped unhurt and got no burns, I thought it was not terrible and dangerous. So I did not stop.'

Old Ra-Ta smiled again and said:
'Yes, my boy. You are wise enough to make the right decision, even when you do not know what's in front of you.'

'Grandpa, why this fire does not burn? Is there a fire that does not burn?'

'Yes, my son, it happens,' Ra-Ta said. 'But in the cave it was not a fire.'

'And what was there?' Horus surprised.
'In the cave it was only a face of the fire, but not the fire itself.'

Horus did not understand. Grandfather continued:
'The fire burns in some other place and its image is transmitted in the cave. What you see is a reality, but it does not exist there. This is like a mirage in the desert. This is not a fire that does not burn. There is also such a fire; it is difficult to call, but priests can do it, although such fire is associated with the forces of the gods and these powers should not be abused. What you've been through was an illusion, it was an image of a fire to test your courage and your determination to reach knowledge. And you have shown that you know how not to be afraid. That's the only meaning of the test.'

For a long time Horus thought about what his grandfather said. And then he asked him:

'Why? The point is just not to be afraid? Afraid of what, grandfather? How can one be afraid of knowledge?'

Grandpa smiled again:

'Yes, my son. Many take knowledge as a burden, not all can withstand it. Only those who feel that they are meant for the knowledge understand that it is their only need. They are not afraid of it. This is the whole point of such test.'

After the first test Horus had to pass the next ones. It happened every two or three years as he was growing. So this time he was again led down into the cave with a labyrinth; again he received same instruction, 'Go along the light and do not slow down.' And he went forth trying not to slacken his pace. Left in the dark alone with his thoughts he recalled the final test, which he passed. He recalled how in the dark he could hear the sounds which normally make people horrified; the voices of wild beasts, some scary and unpleasant touches, growling of predators, who were approaching him.

Then he felt that he was about to be attacked by wild animals and die. It was very scary. He tried to drive these thoughts away, but it did not work because the sound appeared again and again, getting closer and closer, and he understood that he was approaching them himself. Where does he go, what is it? Menagerie? Or some wild cats and lions accidentally got there in the cave? He could not understand it. But since he, as before, was told not to slow down, he did not slow down.

He remembered the most important condition. He was told: 'If you return back, there will be no school for you. You will stay with what you already know. You can serve the country, the people, you can be useful to your motherland, but you will not receive knowledge anymore.' He wanted knowledge. And when fear and doubt crept into his mind, he thought that something might happen: some of these wild animals, who rustled and roared around him in the dark, may indeed attack him. Horus wanted to seek help from the stars, but since he was in the cave, he could not see the stars, and also it was a daytime on the surface, so, without seeing stars he might not be able to call them.

Still he decided he would not turn back, because if he did not go forward, he would lose the opportunity to know all the things that he wanted to know. And without this life had no meaning for him, it was not interesting. Everything else was too easy and clear to him who since childhood accustomed to fight with weapons, to control his body, senses and mind. He was beckoned only with mysterious and unknown, what was dimly perceived in the depths of his soul and could make him to re-gather all his strength, all his attention, all his desires. He strived for it. And he had passed. The sounds of invisible animals were left behind, and he got to that room, which he was supposed to reach.

Horus drove away a series of memories and

noticed with surprise that nothing was happening in darkness anymore. He was walking peacefully. There was no fire, no water, through which he had already recently passed. No sound, no rustling — nothing. It seemed strange. Some light started to gleam ahead. As he was coming up more and more, he saw that it was the door. The end of the corridor was lighted. When he reached it he found that there was a fairly spacious room. There were a table, two chairs and a bed in the room. He stood in amazement and looked around: it seemed he had come, but there was no one there, nobody was meeting him. The corridor ended, darkness was over too. He seemed to fulfill the condition, he didn't give up. And what was the essence of the test?'

Suddenly, he felt someone's presence. He turned in the opposite direction: corridor led further from the room. There was also some kind of passage. He did not know what was there, but because he was told to go to the light he did not go further. Suddenly out of the darkness on the other side a figure of a girl appeared. She was dark-skinned, dressed in transparent clothes. She was holding a cup of some dark beverage. On its surface there were beautifully arranged small buds of roses that have not yet blossomed.

The girl came out of the darkness and stood in front of him, looking at him calmly with her beautiful brown eyes. Horus was surprised, he could not figure out who this girl was, because he was told that, as always, at the end of his trial he would meet his teacher. 'Maybe this girl is also his student,' he thought, 'and she came here before the teacher.' He was ashamed to ask her about it. But after a long pause he realized that she was not going to say it, and he asked: 'Sister, do you know where is our teacher?'

Surprised she told him: 'I have no teachers, young man.'

Horus became even more surprised: if this girl was not a pupil, what was she doing there? And he asked her with surprise: 'Who are you, sister?'

Looking down, the beauty said quietly: 'I bring the award to the winners, make them to forget their worries, and bring them the cup of pleasure...'

'The prize?' though Horus. 'What kind of reward?' He did not even though that he might be worthy of any award. So far he has not done anything in his life, he did not help anyone except for little things for his friends and parents. 'How can there be a reward?' thought Horus. Finally, he began to realize what it all meant. She stood with dropped eyes and waited for him. Only now he appreciated how beautiful she was, though for him it did not matter.

When she put the cup on the table he realized that it was the wine, and finally he understood what was going on. She just invited him to spend time with her. But how was it possible? His teacher was supposed to come here now as he was told. How could he sit there and have fun? Horus immediately pushed these thoughts away and said:

'Sister, I'd be glad to talk to you at another time.

But now I cannot. I'm waiting for my teacher, he is about to come. If you do not learn from him or you do not know him, then what are you doing here?'

She understood everything. She took the cup back and said:

'Nothing. Perhaps I just got lost,' she turned and walked away.

Horus was even more surprised. He remained standing in the middle of the room. He did not even sit down, and he could not imagine, he could not understand why there were these chairs and why was the bed. How could he become so tired that he would need a bed? 'And what if I will have to wait here till morning?' he thought. He walked from corner to corner and was expecting that his teacher, to whom he came, should still come out.

Time went on, but the teacher did not show up. After about an hour he heard the approaching steps and quiet rustle that came from different places. After a few minutes twelve young students like him but a little older, dressed in white, stood in front of him. They looked unperturbed, no one said anything. They surrounded him in silence and turned their faces in the direction of the corridor. And then they started to move.

Horus was in the center. He realized that he should go with them. He already walked at a different pace, not as when he was passing down the corridor before. Gradually he began to understand what was happening. After a couple of hundred steps, turning to the side, the twelve disciples went along with him in a big beautiful room — it was a sanctuary of Isis. There stood the priests dresses in the same white robes. In the depths of the hall there was a large bronze statue of the goddess with the golden rose on the chest and with a diadem on her head. In her arms she held her son Horus. Looking at this statue, Horus thought with wonder of his parents, who gave him the name.

Right beneath the statue stood a priest in a purple dress.The priest approached Horus and said: 'You've passed the test. You have shown that you can control your lower nature. You have fulfilled the main condition. But in order to know the truth, you have to take an oath of silence. Are you ready, my son?' asked a senior priest.

'Yes, Father,' said Horus and respectfully bowed his head.

'Then repeat after me: Let my name be erased from the book of life...'

Horus repeated: 'Let my name be erased from the book of life. Let all my deeds be erased from the memory of men and gods. Let the memories about me be eliminated on the Earth and in the Universe. Let nobody learns about my name or my place. And let me not to see life anymore if I violate my oath...'

Horus quietly repeated: '... If I break my oath, if I disclose the mystery to those who are not worthy or to those who are not from the circle of my teachers and their students.'

Then one of the priests in white robes who were standing on the side, walked up to him, and the senior priest said to Horus:

'Here's your new teacher. Follow him and he will disclose to you the secrets that you already are worthy to know. But remember about his vow of silence.

Horus gave a nod toward the older, and after his new teacher.

19. The Daughter of a Priest

Absorbed in thoughts Horus was going home from the temple. He thought about how times were changed. He realized that he had grown up, and it was not exactly as he used to imagine before. Up until now he used to get clear knowledge: 'This word is such. That sign is such. It means this.'

Then the deeper meaning of concepts was revealed to him. One day, when he was hearing the explanation on the sky structure, Horus asked his new teacher about the names of the constellations:

'Holy Father, who divided the constellations and named them?'

'My son, sages keep covenants of gods since time immemorial. They explained to people how the whole universe arranged.'

'I remember it, Father. But I'm surprised by their outline. Here, for example, the constellations of Taurus or Leo, as well as others, do not resemble the shape of these animals at all. By drawing lines from one star to the other one can draw very different figures. Why the gods and sages decided to call them that?'

The teacher smiled slightly:

'Horus, only ignorant people and small children think that the constellations are so named because they resemble the silhouettes of animals. Each star like everything else in the cosmos emits specific rays at the entire Universe. The rays of some of these stars are similar in their properties, while others are different. Only the highest sages know all kinds of light and the energies that these stars emit. It takes a lifespan for a human to conceive even a part of this knowledge. Vibrations that emanate from heaven are involved in the creation of life forms on Earth. Each kind of higher energies has its different manifestations. For example, the creative power of the rays of Taurus constellation is most expressed in those who were born under the Taurus. The same with others. The constellation of Taurus has a special creative power. That's why it is first in the list, and the count of a stellar year every 26 000 years begins with it. Moreover, for a human it is easier to remember shapes and names that are familiar to him since childhood. That is why the constellations have names of animals.

Horus began to understand that each symbol has unfathomable and deep knowledge. His teacher said that every nation on Earth began with temples devoid of images and even symbols. Only when the memory of the great truths and the original Wisdom given to the mankind by the dynasties of divine kings, worn off, people had to resort to memos and symbolism. For hours Horus studied big scrolls of the sacred tables, which referred to the conformity of all that was on the ground with what was in the sky. There were the names of different stones, plants, metals, visible colors and audible sounds as well as what luminaries they all match. Horus memorized everything. He could not take these tables home; he could not even speak about them in the presence of strangers. These all were the strictest secrecies, which he, like all those who had passed, swore to keep once and for all. To violate this oath meant death. He was instructed how, in practice, one can apply these powers, by what methods one can call them, collect and direct. Then the instructions decreased, and he was given the opportunity to apply the new knowledge in practice. The more he understood what was described in the books and tables, the less specific instructions his teachers gave him. He had to think more on his own, ask questions, not out loud, but in his mind, and wait until the answer came. Then he had to ponder over the answer, and if it was not convincing or seemed wrong, he asked the question again to receive a new answer. Then he tried to apply it in his life and then ask a new question. This went on again and again.

Horus did not really understand what was happening to him and where he was going, but it was the way that he himself had chosen, and he had to go through it to the very end as at the time of testing.

Lost in thought, he did not notice that he'd covered all the distance to the house. Only after he had entered the courtyard, he saw that his father was talking to some strangers, and the appearance and clothing of these people were obviously not from these parts.

Father happily introduced his son to the guests. Clearly he was proud of him. It turned out that the guests were also priests. They were from Aztlan country and they had to live for some time in their home, because more and more people were coming and there was no place for them. These priests arrived for some work and had to return to their home after. The king had to host the guests among his courtiers and military leaders.

Horus bowed respectfully. He caught a glimpse of something surprisingly familiar in the eyes of one of the priests, even though he had never seen him before, but his penetrating gaze seemed to be very familiar and somewhat allied. Horus went into the house in silence. Mother was preparing food for all. Two servants, who probably came with the guests, helped her. Having entered a large room on the first floor, he was surprised to see two women siting there. By their appearance and dress they resembled to the priest, whom he had seen in the yard. He guessed that they were probably his relatives, maybe even his family. A moment later he could distinguish them even better.

One woman was an adult, she was older than his mother. Her features reflected her natural beauty, her eyes emanated the same mind and insight which he noticed in a priest of Aztlan. Beside her sat a young girl. Apparently, she was her daughter. The mother called her own name and the name of her daughter. Horus also politely introduced himself.

And then, when Horus looked at her more closely, something happened. He could not understand what was happening to him. He must have gotten bewildered. But for a while he clearly realized that in his mind there were no thoughts at all. He looked at her in surprise. She was so beautiful that he just stopped breathing.

Then he again tried to understand what was happening to him. His legs were somewhere far away; they reported to the head from below that they were unable to move; they were jammed and would stand until they receive an order. The heart beat quickened, and his mind, which could not answer his questions, was frantically looking for some answer. Horus could not understand what was he looking for. Then he realized: his mind was trying to understand who he could compare this girl with. He tried to remember all the statues of goddesses, bas-reliefs of queens and beautiful women and images of women in general that he had seen. He tried to remember all that remained in his memory and could not find anything alike.

This girl was absolutely not in comparison with anybody or anything. He realized it when his mind came to the very end of his unsuccessful digging in the archives of memory and reported that it could not find anything like it, and that it was powerless in this case. Then to his surprise Horus saw soft bluish light that came as if from somewhere above and some silent voice or rather some thought together with this light crept into his soul. And this silent voice said to him: 'Do not worry; you'll be okay with her.'

Only then Horus realized what awkward position he was in, standing in the middle of the room and looking in surprise at people who were guests of his family. He thought that it was probably disrespectful: to stand and look at them for so long. He gave them a courteous nod and went upstairs with his scrolls. But then, when he sat in his room and opened the scrolls, he realized that he saw nothing in there: no words, no pictures, no images or symbols. The girl kept standing in his eyes although she was still downstairs. In his head he heard her name told by girl's mother — Una.

20. Holiday in Peose

After dinner the guards told the prisoners that the work should finish early today. They all went back into the yard. Then they were told that it was a special day, a great holiday, so Afteb must take the most senior male members of his family and to bring the gifts of the host to the people of Peos.

Afteb called the eldest son, the eldest nephew and the oldest son-in-law and together they all went into the barns of the host. The guards rolled out some other carts. They never saw such carts: these were clean and stylish, with patterns, bound with metal from different sides and had some inscriptions on them. Then they loaded various kinds of fruit onto each cart, and, accompanied by only one of the host's warriors, who showed them the way, they went to the city center.

There was a festive atmosphere in the town in spite of the usual anxiety. People of Aztlan knew how to have fun. They loved rest and joy. Many people with families, with friends and relatives were walking through the streets. They stopped, talked, joked and laughed.

And so, looking at the passers-by, the slaves reached the city center. There at the square a guard showed them the place: here should stand three trucks, and they must stand by in silence. Each passer-by can take some fruits if he wants, because it is the treat of their boss. Today is a special holiday; today is the Moon-goddess's Festival.

Then, the guard told them a strange phrase, which was not very clear to them: ' Well, perhaps you will find the way back', and retired.

He made a few steps forward, turned around and added:
'If you lose your way, come back to this place, I will come for you in the morning again.'

So, the guard left. Afteb and older men of his family were left to stand in the square quietly looking at passers-by. People came from all directions. They flowed from different streets into the city center. There were many people in colorful robes at the square. The prisoners were surprised to see many beautiful women, many different outfits and patterns on them. Somewhere in the distance, where the square came to an end and the park began, there were some amusement devices whirling in the air with cheerful kids. A little later these devices which looked like big spinning mill raised in the air, went down; the kids got out of them, and others got in, and again there was merry hustle and bustle.

Afteb stood with his boys in the square throughout the night. Passers-by were coming up, choosing fruit to their taste, handing them over to share with others, and enjoyed. Sometimes they remembered the host's name, thanked and moved away.

Toward sunset, when the sun and the sky in the west grew red, the servants heard some noise on the other side of the square. The plaza was huge and they did not see it all because some buildings closed their review. When the noise increased, the crowd moved there, and soon the noise stopped and the music began to sound instead. The music was loud and very peculiar. It contained unusual rhythms. Sometimes the unusual sounds resembling the sounds of nature, loud and slow, were heard in it.

Fascinated members of the Afteb's family looked at this spectacle, all but himself — he looked away. He looked to where the street went on. There stood a house, like a castle. It was the home of the head city ruler. Just above it the sun was setting.

Soon darkness fell, and the lights were lit in the square. The lights always lit at night regardless of whether it was in the days of festivals and ordinary days; they always turn on in the dark. The sound of music grew, more and more people came to the square, they continued to come back and take the fruit.

This lasted for a few hours. Then the moon began to rise over the city. The crowd enthusiastically listened to the musicians. The musicians were alternating and so was the music as well as the dance. Sometimes the whole crowd became like a single organism. It began to move in a circle while performing different dance movements. Sometimes it again dissolved and turned into a mass; people were just listening to the music. Then, when musicians again played something rhythmic and inspiring, the crowd once again would turn into a large group of dancers. Sometimes this mass of people loudly sang along with the melody of the song. But then vice versa everyone went silent and listened to the singer, and sometimes the music was without words and voices.

This could last probably until the morning, but most of the people in the crowd felt tired by the middle of the night. People slowly began to disperse. Some people remained on the square until the end.

Afteb and his family did not know what to do.

They probably would have to wait until the end of this festival, especially because not all fruits were over and some refreshments were not yet taken by the people. They saw that the more and more people were leaving the area. They were very tired themselves, they wanted to sleep, and they remembered that again they would have to work tomorrow. Therefore the young eventually persuaded the old man that it was better to go home. The owner will not be angry, and also guards were not there with them today. This latest news was the most amazing for them. It means their owners trusted them so much that they could easily let them go even without guards or leave them in the city.

Afteb was also tired, therefore he agreed to the entreaties of the young and decided to turn back. They took the carts and drove home. Fortunately the road was easy; they made just two turns and they did not forget what way they came from. On their way back the men noticed sadness on the face of the old man. The nephew asked him: 'Uncle Afteb, are you very tired? Why are you sad?'

The old man waited and then said thoughtfully: 'I've never seen such celebrations and such fun. In our village, when people were going to have fun everything was much simpler and poorer... But I'd give a lot to see it again, but not this. I guess I'm not destined to see my native land.'

'What are you saying, uncle Afteb,' protested the nephew. 'We pray to our gods every night, and we should believe that they will help us.'

'Yes, Tamil, they will help us. And if I will not be able to return to our homeland, may the gods help you, so that at least you can see it.' In this way, having such sad discussion, they reached the master's house, brought the carts with the remaining fruit again in the barn and returned to their beds. All their relatives have long been asleep.'

21. The Great Test

The heavy door of the cave closed with a dull sound behind his back, and on the floor, as it had happened before, there was thin and even strip of light, pointing him the way. Horus focused on his feelings for a moment and noticed that this time he was totally free from excitement or anxiety. He perceived everything clearly, simply, and wisely, as his teacher would say. And he wasn't absolutely bothered that the whole world around him was plunged into darkness. He moved forward along the stream of light. His steps were measured but fairly quick as in his previous tests, but this time none of the priests said to him that he should go without slowing the pace down. Soon having gone a little bit more he realized why the streak of light broke in the dark. And he stopped. He felt someone's presence and waited. Soon he heard slow steps; they approached him and stopped somewhere in a few meters from him. Horus realized that it was the beginning of the first of the great trials.

He heard the voice in complete darkness: 'Brother, what are you looking for here?'

It was obviously the voice of one of the older priests. The voice seemed a little familiar. He heard it somewhere at the great ceremonies attended by many priests. Perhaps one of the Hierophants stood before him, but he had no time to remember whose voice it was, he had to answer: 'I seek for wisdom, Father.'

The voice asked again after a short pause: 'Who do you want to find it from, o seeker?'

'From the sages of Egypt, who store the knowledge of the gods, a teacher.'

The voice paused again, then it asked: 'My son, If you met any of the sages on your way, who realized the legacy of gods and the laws of the Universe, what would you ask him about?'

Now it was Horus turn to pause. Horus collected

his thoughts, wondering what question to ask, and then spoke.

'O, keeper of wisdom, I would ask him why small is like great, and why what is above is similar to what is at the bottom?'

Priest asked without pause: 'And what do you think?'

Horus decided not to hide his guesses: 'Because all of them are parts of the One.'

'Great answer, my son. What more do you want to know?'

There was no irony or condescension in the priest's voice. Horus felt his complete kindness and respect, even though Horus knew that he suited to be his son or even grandson. For a moment he hesitated; so much he wanted to know and now he got permission for that. What to ask?

'Tell me, Father, why do people, who also belong to the One, see, feel and understand everything so differently? Why do they remember the One only vaguely and call each other brothers and sisters only because of common parentage? Also I would like to understand the words of the great Toth in three Worlds: 'The universe is a circle in which the center is everywhere and the circumference is nowhere.'

After a brief silence the invisible priest spoke again out of the darkness: 'My son, If you and your brother stood in a certain location on the banks of the Nile, but he would be back to you and to the river, what would each of you see?'

Horus thought he got the idea of the sage and replied: 'I would see the river and its other shore, o teacher, and my brother would see only the fields and rocks. He would not see the Great River.'

'You see, my son, this is the case with everything in this world. When two persons stand next to each other and look at one point, what they see will be similar. And when they look back, they see something quite different. And this is true to all the people who stand at the same spot but with a few exceptions they all stand with their back to the One. Therefore only those who are very close to each other have similar vision. Others see something completely different. But to know the One, even if we are in it, we should not stand with our back to it. And what do you think, seeker?'

Horus has grasped the meaning of simple and profound analogy of the priest. It dawned upon him: 'To see everything, we should stand with our back to everything else but the One. The one we should face. I understand your wise advice. Only then can we see what everyone see and we can see what others do not see. I always felt that the One is in me. Thank you, Father!'

Then he paused and said quietly: 'But how can we see the One?'

The sage's reply was slow and a bit more solemn

than before: 'Obviously, you can do it by standing next to one who has realized Him and looking to where the knower looks. But how to be around if you are away?'

The young man lost in thought. He understood that the question itself contains the answer: 'When my mother, my father and teacher are far away I see them in my mind and I feel that they are close. I feel that even my grandfather, Ra-Ta, is close to me although I have not seen him before when I was small. That time he lived far away from the river head of the Nile, but I remember well that his spirit was close. I did not even know his face, but often it seemed that I felt his presence and that I saw him. Then, when I saw him for the first time, I was surprised that his appearance was exactly what I imagined being a young child. This means it is all about thought, wise master?'

'Yes, my son, the essence is thought and remembering the image of a person to whom we are committed.'

Horus understood everything, but inspired by the kindness of the priest, unexpectedly even for himself he said: 'You, Father, spoke so wisely about the One. You certainly know Him. How can I be with you? My parents and all those who knew him used to tell me about my grandfather. But I am very ashamed that I know nothing about you. And I have never even seen your image close...'

Whether because of a bit contrite-sounding voice of Horus in the mood of prayer and reverence touched the sage, or because it should have been like this, but the wise man calmly replied: 'It is not difficult to fix my son...'

And in that same moment all of a sudden a bright light poured from above and lit up the whole figure of the speaker. In astonishment Horus recognized the very Hept Safty in him — Grand Hierophant, who was supreme over all the priests and the chief advisor of the Pharaoh. He immediately remembered the scenes of celebrations, when he saw Hierophant from afar and heard his voice. It was said that he had conquered even old age and death and can live as long as he decides himself. Horus stood humbly clenched hands in a gesture of gratitude, but he could not bow his head at the same time. He peered intently into the face of the Hierophant trying to get a better view of his appearance. The sage's eyes poured out the wonderful and gentle light on the young man. A powerful but lite and bright whirlwind caught his spirit and seemed to lift him high to the invisible source of light pouring from above. He remembered when in his childhood his father took him in his arms, threw him up and then caught the delighted baby in the air. Now he felt something very similar; he did not take his eyes off the great Hierophant, who also watched him closely and friendly and also did not take his gaze away. For the second time in his life Horus I saw a man with such radiant and glowing glance. Previously it seemed to him that the only person in the world who owned such a glance was his grandfather, the wisest of the wise. But his grandfather never looked for so long directly in the eyes of anyone as if not wanting to surprise people with his strength. Looking at the great sage Hept-Saft Horus now began to understand better what power actually his grandfather had. But then it was all over. The lights went out, and he heard how the sound of same slow steps was moving away from him until finally it completely faded away. Joyful and a little confused Horus was still in the same darkness and did not know what to do next. Then he heard footsteps again, which again began to approach him. And then for some reason he felt the excitement for the first time in the day. The steps just as well have stopped somewhere in the ten cubits from him. But this time the voice was obviously belonged to someone else. Horus wondered how they could walk so easily in the complete darkness. He could see nothing but he heard a new question: 'My brother, what are you doing here?'

He responded without concealing his joy: 'Holy Father, I just talked to the great Hierophant.'

The voice continued: 'How did you know that it was him?'

'I recognized his noble face and heard his voice. He spoke so wisely and he was so kind to me. He honored me by allowing me to ask questions and answered them.'

However, the priest speaking in the dark did not agree with him: 'Why do you believe that it was he and not someone else?'

'The Holy Father, it was a great gift to me. You

want me to refuse such a gift and to think that it was only an illusion?'

The voice replied calmly: 'I just want you to think, my son. Maybe it was someone else?'

Horus naively surprised:
'Why, Father? I recognized his face and remembered his voice.'

The priest continued with restrain: 'My young brother, haven't you seen skilled actors who, putting on a mustache and a beard and paint on their faces can be like any other man? Haven't you not heard of jokers who at banquets can parrot someone else's voices, they can parody even the voice of the pharaoh, the ruler of Egypt? They can say anything, so that the audience bursts out laughing. You are still young, but didn't you see that? Why do you believe that you saw and heard the great Hierophant when any of these jokers could easily forge his appearance, and his voice?'

Horus confused. But since the priest was waiting, he had to say something. And he said: 'Yes, Father, you are right. Skilled mummers can depict any person. They can even remember and repeat his words as well as to change them if they want it. But can they pain on their own faces the light of his eyes or the beauty of his soul and the greatness of his heart? Are there such paints in all of Egypt? How can they depict his spirit if it is great? To represent wisdom they must have it themselves. But though I am young, Father, I never heard sages engaging in such buffoonery.

Rather, they are always serious. And even the most kind of them sometimes seem severe and harsh. Therefore only the one who is great could depict the great. Is there in Egypt the second chief Hierophant?'

Horus was silent. It seemed to him that the silence had disappeared and there were still some people around him. After a short pause the priest told him: 'You've answered me, brother. Peace to you.

Then steps began to move off. When they died away, Horus again noticed some light somewhere at the top. He looked up, but when he saw a beam of light flowing from above, his eyes that have already accustomed to the darkness, instinctively squinted. He lowered his head and stood there for a few moments. But when he opened his eyes again he was surprised to find himself in the center of illuminated and spacious room. There were no signs or letters on the walls. Everything was very strict and simple. Smooth rectangular columns without any patterns formed a perfect circle around. Behind them on a small hill there were large wooden chairs that looked like thrones. Horus looked around and saw that about a dozen of priests sat in these chairs at the equal distance from him. Surprised, he looked and recognized the faces of all present. They were all senior priests and Hierophants. Right in front of him sat the great Hierophant and looked straight in his eyes. Horus was again looking at him, but then he thought that it was not very polite and, folding his arms, he bowed his head in a sign of respect. Again he heard footsteps and when he looked up he saw that Hierophant himself again was moving directly towards him, but this time light was on. When the oldest stopped, another priest came holding a large and beautiful cup in his hand. Hierophant with all his majesty looked at him with approval. And Horus again heard his voice: 'You can fool the eyes and ears, but nothing can cheat the heart. The wise see with their heart, hear with the heart. Nothing unclean will affect the heart, for the sword trusted to them is sharpened.'

Horus listened in surprise, and the sage continued: 'You have passed the test, the seeker. Now everyone, even the older and wiser, despite your young age, shall call you brother. Rejoice, our brother, your spirit won today!'

Horus suddenly thought for a moment, what a pity was that his grandfather did not see him now. He would be happy and proud of his grandson. He suddenly realized how much he would like to please his grandfather, whom he loved as much as his mother and father.

Hierophant took the cup from the hands of an assistant, came up to Horus and showed it to him. The cup was full of red drink. The young man again reverently bowed his head and heard his words: 'Receive and drink your cup. Drain it to see the mystery of the bottom.'

At the bottom was a picture of the prostrate man, enclosed in the circle of the serpent, and the words: 'You are a giver of everything and a receiver of everything.'

22. The Road

Iltar and Wotan in their Vimana are waiting for the appointed time of negotiations. A long distance mirror on the board is switching on and they talk to Las-lu, the governor of the city Sas and a member of the council of Emperor Alta. Las Lu says that it is time to hit the road to the west across the whole ocean. Iltar asks: 'Who then stays here with Pharaoh Araar-art?'

'Tomorrow at dawn, a new and the largest group of builders is flying to the land of Egypt where they will start to build a new city for our people, in which our rulers will also live. They are led by one of the senior advisors of the lord, Kurnovuu. So Arar-rat can always talk directly with our master.'

Realizing that with such a representative there is just no need in ambassador, Iltar asks a new question: 'Where do we go and what should we do at the other side of the ocean?'

'You will go at the isthmus to Mayyapanu in Yucatan. Hundreds of thousands of our people will be able to arrive on ships and vimanas in the Nile Valley, but the remaining millions need a way over land. When the lords of wisdom warn us about the storm, there will be no time for packing. Maya leaders are ready to accept us, but all those who will go to the land of Myra and Amaruku must also pass through their country. It is necessary to quickly build a road. It must be made of durable stone and be at least a hundred cubits wide like our main routes between cities on Poseidonis, which are illuminated throughout day and night. The road to the land of Myra is already being built, and the road to Mayapan will be made by you. The builders with machines have already come there by the sea, and those who were closer, came by land. Today at sunset they will begin to go ashore. Wotan and you must catch up with them and manage the overall operation.'

'How far will the road extend?'

'As far as you can do in a month. This will be the main way. Our migrants will continue your work. There is a dense forest everywhere, and it will be necessary to construct tracks leading to all the big villages and towns of our colonists. And be careful; in the forests live not only our brothers Maya but also dark-skinned savages who prey on people. Watch must be both day and night. Therefore we sent twice as many soldiers together with our builders' squad. Hurry up, my brothers, and may the One help you!'

After a talk with a counselor Iltar and Wotan go down into the house where they lived, pack their bags and say goodbye to the hospitable hosts. Then, climbing into a sparkling machine, they soar into the sky and head to the west.

The next morning after having discussed the overall plan with the builders they start to work. Iltar looks over the impassable thicket of the primeval forest, then goes down to the softly humming machines and monitors the process. A young operator knows his job pretty well. He says to Iltar that to control their installations they use them together with the currents of space and energy of the human. Therefore due to the presence of particularly empowered people they will work even better. Then the operator turns on the device which starts to hum quietly.

Stones of different sizes and types manifest in the air within a radius of hundreds of elbows. Large and small, completely losing their weight, they are light like feathers. Driven by the wind they gradually approach the site and gather in a big pile. The man behind the remote runs a hand over the device. The sound changes and becomes lower. The pile of stones in the air begins to stretch in length and gets down to earth. With the new movement of the operator the sound change is added with the crunch of twigs on the ground and a loud crack of rocks. All this huge and stretched out mass of stones becomes many times heavier, and under its own monstrous weight comparable to a giant press, the rocks start to sink into the ground and into each other, crushing the trunks even the strongest trees to the very root. After almost a half of this mass is pushed into the ground, the operator turns off the device and gets down. Another smaller car run by other more senior operator slowly takes off. Upon reaching the rock mass it begins to emit a thin and piercing ringing.

Wotan also supervises the work. He knows that this sound is dangerous only where it is directed and focused. Nevertheless, feeling slight pain, he covers his ears and backs away. When the small machine reaches the end portion, the whistling ring stops. Young operator returns to his instruments and the entire upper half of already well-fitted and almost monolithic stone mass, separated from the bottom, slowly begins to rise into the air. Reaching the height slightly higher than its width, the mass hangs in the air and, directed by the man in the machine, slowly turns in the air. When the 180-degree turn is over and all smoothly cut faces are not at the bottom as before the rise but already at the top, the machine along with rows of stones hanging in the air begins to move forward on already laid rows of masonry. When it reaches the end, the sound changed again, and the whole mass begins to descend. Again there is frequent crunch of twigs on the ground and loud cracks of stones, and all this mass evenly undercut from the top again becomes many times heavier. Under its own weight it is pressed into the earth and into each other until only a small protruding portion, precisely docked in height and breadth with the previous section. The first machine pulls back and vacates the nearly finished section of the road to give way to the third machine, which is also smaller, but has two long strips protruding on both sides that precisely moved apart to a desired width.

Again the high whistling ring starts. Rough edges of masonry are cut and fall off. Iltar and Wotan, as instructors, examine the finished site, measure the width. If they don't find significant flaws, they send the first three machines to work further, where they start the entire process again from the very beginning. The machines are followed by other two even smaller machines. The first one, stopping at regular intervals after four cubits, drills round holes the size of a open palm in the rock mass, and the second machine inserts white balls made of shatterproof safety glass. The balls protrude outwards by half of their size. When finished on the right side, they then repeat the same steps on the left one. When the entire first section is done and the balls are stacked in place, operators return to the beginning and start a stand-alone small device. After a while all the balls start to emit soft matte light.

This went on day after day for several weeks, and the road was increasing, reaching deep into the country. All builders' squad together with security, machinery and viman was moving every day to the edge of the already finished road. At night the light of inextinguishable lamps was already visible a long way around. At the beginning of the third week a granite rock stood directly in their path. It was carefully examined for the direction of its cracks, then gently raised, turned in the right direction and smoothly cut into several layers which were laid along the road under construction. In the process of laying new cracks manifested, but everything was so perfectly tailored that the construction did not lose its strength at all.

Iltar and Votan monitored the course of the work as usual until one night they felt a strange anxiety. From a young age, when they both were taught by the wise priests, they were accustomed to trust their misgivings, but this time they shared with each other and made sure that it was something serious; they could not understand what could happen and what should they do. Then Iltar remembered about the warning given to him before the departure of Las lu. He called his friend into viman, suggested him to turn Sushumna on and lifted the apparatus to a small height. Below it was already dark. The device that detects even slightest reflections of moonlight in the darkness showed a large concentration of some bodies in the woods under the trees not far to the north of them. Without turning the exterior lights on the pilots silently moved their winged vehicle there and began to watch this place from the top:

'Look, Wotan! These are hunters. Why are they here?'

'Yes, there is a whole army of them! Elephants do not inhabit these areas for a long time. So who else will they hunt in the dark of night?'

Then they both were flashed with a guess: 'Gee! This is what we've sensed! We must warn our people!'

'Yes, my friend, the human is better than any machine. But if we release Mash-Mac here, it will melt our road and burn the whole forest! Besides they have much more soldiers than we. What to do?'

'Here, brother Wotan, we need a magical sound that collects stones but only retroactively. When I studied in Alta, we were explained how to use it in fight for protection. This is the best thing that we have now.'

23. Defense

While coming back they see on the screen that the crowd at the bottom begins to move toward their camp. They land their vimana near the camp and both jump out of it and hastily run to their people. Wotan comes up to the guards and says that they are just about to be attacked. But savages are moving out of the woods, therefore they should use lightning rods only as a last resort, because the fire will devour the trees and burn down the whole neighborhood. Iltar calls a young operator of the stone-collecting machine and orders to quickly turn the sound so that it gives the opposite effect and covers only their entire camp. The device lights up with green and yellow lights in the dark and begins to hum softly. The white light from the glass spheres illuminates a small area of the forest, behind which reigns a complete darkness. The warriors notice some movement in the forest only when the first ranks of hunters go out to the illuminated edge of the forest. No sooner the savages appear out of the darkness with bows and arrows at the ready, they begin to shoot. Light whistling of a large number of arrows gives courage to the attackers until some of them are struck with the same number of arrows. Wounded, gritting their teeth out of pain, they are surprised to see that these were their own arrows. When they look closer at the red-skinned warriors standing on the road, they do not find them holding any sort of bows and arrows. Not only the red-faced are not shooting, but they are not moving, too. As far as purpose of the objects that they hold in their hands at the ready, the attackers have no idea about it. Wotan comes up to the cordon of soldiers at the edge of the road. He sees that some of the arrows that did not turn back or did not fly over an arc of the invisible barrier are hanging in the air quivering as if in the wind. These are arrows with the tips made not of stone but of bone. Pure white light of illumination reflecting in the leaves of trees acquires a greenish hue. Despite the fact that the sun had already set, a mass of mosquitoes and other insects spins in the air. Wotan raises his hand, pointing his men to the frozen arrows. The soldiers, who at first thought the familiar sounds of machines and devices were usual work and did not notice their influence on the result of the shooting at their side, come to the edge of the road and to their surprise look at the unusual sight. They share quietly among each other that they did not even know that the construction machinery could be used in such a way. Truly wisdom is above any weapon.

Seeing that nothing is achieved the attackers decide to attack again but this time with all their strength. They rush to the lighted camp, but just before reaching the place where the trees end, they are stopped by some unseen force that was beating and burning their naked bodies. Affected by such an unknown weapon, many of them fall to the ground, while others stand as if rooted to the ground unable to move. Watching the unusual battle between the savages and his machine, Iltar ordered the operator to gradually expand the range of the protective sound action. As a result, those who came out of the woods are pushed back under the trees. And the further the invisible and burning strength drives them, the more it becomes visible in the dark. Retreating under its pressure the crowd of hunters begin to see how it glows in the dark. It resembles a thin wall made of light that shimmers with different colors of fire.

Realizing that their weapons do not go to any comparison with the magical power of the aliens lording in their lands, savages eventually back down and dissolve into their forests. Iltar orders to leave the protection turned on until the dawn. Now they will have to do it every night to avoid unnecessary risk. He then takes off in the sky in his vimana again to make sure that the enemy is completely cleared, and only then he allows his men to rest. Returning to the cabin to turn off the navigation instruments, he is surprised to see that another device with the night lights switched off is circling at a low altitude not far to the north from their place. Wotan also wonders who could it be from their island? If they flew to them, they would have been warned in advance. Sensing that something was wrong the pilots, too, alike a strange night scout do not turn the lights on and again soar into the sky to watch a stranger. Considering the fact that the strangers do not in any way react to their approach they conclude that that is not a combat machine, but an ordinary or business one, which is devoid of devices for identifying other vehicles in the air. Such vimanas cannot see others in the dark unless the latest go directly towards them.

Looking at Sushumna the old Zuluum says to Chaakunu: 'Why did these forest dwellers launch this night hunting?'

'Maybe they have a holiday, Father?'

But the old man's intuition suggests something very different:
'There cannot be a holiday without lights, my son. They hunted someone in the dark, but now they are returning to their huts. We'll have to wait until they fall asleep.'

Half an hour later the movement at the bottom stops. Viman lands quietly on the meadow. Atlanteans instantly get off and burst into two nearest huts. Those who managed to grab weapons they stun by a blow on their heads, bound them all, put them on the shoulders and quickly return to viman, which gently rises into the air and heads to the northeast.'

Iltar thoughtfully follows them with his eyes: 'Aren't they those bandits, who frequented the lands of Araar-aart?'

Wotan sadly continues his thought: 'And they disgraced our nation in the entire country... Did you see who this viman belongs to?'

'I did, brother Wotan. It is viman of Zuluum from the town of Peos. It seems to me that when Pharaoh decides to search again for his people he will find them there. And the slaves from Egypt will point to Zuluum. We'll talk about it with Las-Lu tomorrow. Let him tell our lord.'

'Yes, my friend, it was not an easy day. Praise to the One that we timely sensed the enemy and saved our people.'

'Yes, Wotan, and praise to our wise teachers that taught us how to hear the voice of the One and understand the whisper of leaves in the breeze. And if it is not for their blessed wisdom, then we all with of our powerful weapons and machines would have become worse than the poor forest savages like these nocturnal robbers from Peos. Praise to the teachers who taught us the Law of the One... Let's go rest, my friend...'

The next morning when the sun rises over the Mayapan forest, and singing birds begin their flight, the entire camp of the builders, who are weary from their night anxieties, continues to sleep to a soft hum of the running machine. Even guards are asleep under its reliable protection. An hour after the dawn Maya elders from nearby villages come to Iltaru. They have already learned from their scouts about the night attack. They show drawings made by artists according to eyewitnesses' descriptions. They say that these savages are not only different from their people by their darker skin, which has a light brown and slightly reddish hue, but also are very dangerous; they are always ready to steal maize and attack villages. They are said to eat people sometimes. The guests can see a lot of broken arrows scattered around, and they were surprised to notice that builders, who start to work again as if nothing had happened, do not have any wounds and even scratches. They are happy that their brothers from Aztlan have taught a good lesson to these nocturnal robbers. Actually Maya people think that the savages should be driven away in the deep forest, away from the places inhabited by the people with straight eyes and those who follow the One Law. Iltar says they only have to finish the road, and then it will be up to the settlers together with the leaders of Maya to decide what to do with all of these savages. Then he asks one of them: 'Leader Hunak, what kind of people these savages are? If their ancestors were from the educated and those who were faithful to the Law of the Toltecs, they would never eat people. But even though it was hard to see at night, we noticed that they also do not resemble rmoahalas. Rmoahalas have more hair on the bodies. They do not have foreheads and so their heads are round and look like an eggs. But these do have foreheads, though very low and sloping. Eggheads live in the north and in the south. They have not yet reached these places. What kind of race their ancestors belonged to? Are they from tlavatlas, aren't they?'

'My son, tlavatlas have not fallen so low. These narrow-headed are people of Turan. They are eternally at odds with yours and my ancestors, the Toltecs.

Wotan, who was silently listening to their conversation, exclaims: 'They are turans who have turned into barbarians! Long before Aztlan became an island of Ruta and then shrank down to Poseidonis alone, turans had all the time been trying to multiply in order to win skillful and wise Toltecs by their numerical superiority. They even announced that their people can have children and do not even think about them but give them to the rulers who would train them as soldiers. Their leaders used to tell mothers and women, 'Beget, beget more children, and then we all win.' The outcome was that their youth did not want to create families, and street children used to become thieves and robbers. If previously they were just rude Turanians, now they sunk so deep that they lived in the woods like real savages.'

Chief Hunak answers: 'Truly, the one who is cruel to his children is an enemy of all. He dooms his descendants to savagery and brutality. You gave them a good lesson that strength is not in numbers and weapons, but in wisdom and knowledge. And although you have not made them smarter, henceforward they, like wild beasts, will be afraid to attack you. Why didn't you use your Ksiukoatli? Why did you not send against them your fiery serpents?'

'Because the rods of lightning could cause a fire and burn down the whole forest.'

'It was wisely, our brothers, to act carefully. None of you were even hurt with their poisonous arrows. Thank the gods!'

The elders finally say that they will order their scribes to write down for the descendants the glorious history of this night fight. Then they say goodbye and return to their homes.

PART 4

24. The Greatest Initiation

The sun was going to set, and its beams tinged a shiny surface of the pyramids with pink-orange light, which contrasted beautifully with surrounding greenery and the blue of the darkening sky. What striking and unearthly skill could create this miracle of spirit and thought, expressed in stone? This beauty and grandeur scene inspired Horus to stop and to continuously look at it. He has never seen the pyramids, especially so close. But the priests and novices who led him did not stop, so he went along with them. Giant and glittering man-made mountains became closer. Just a few hundred steps before them the procession turned aside, then passed through a gate and began to descend into the underground hall...

Horus saw how passages of the Great Pyramid opened before him, and he remembered the picture with a human body lying horizontally and his soul winged upright hovering above it and realizing everything. He felt that now he was in exactly the same condition. He was experiencing a pleasant feeling in his body. It was obviously the effect of the herbal mixture he was rubbed with. He wanted to remember the composition of the mixture, but out of seven its parts he could now remember only four: rose oil, peanut oil, cedar oil and almond milk...

While the older priests solemnly recited the prayer, the younger ones rubbed his body with the woolen cloth and a fragrant composition. Then they swaddle him up with white linen bandages like a dead man and then put him on a stretcher with a large image of the Egyptian cross Tau and carried him deep into the pyramid. Moreover, sometimes it seemed to him as if the stretcher moved on its own and priests, who walked by his sides barely touched them. He heard a lingering and beautiful sound that resembled a soft whistle or a distant bell, which gradually grew. He had a complete clarity of consciousness, and very soon he realized that the whole thing was the Kaa or an etheric lookalike. His teachers explained to him that at night during the normal sleep the soul leaves the earthly body and wanders in space in the same way as it happens after death. But there is a big difference between sleep and death. At night the Kaa of a person, which contains his vital force, stays with the earthly body, otherwise the body starts to decay and die.

In the time of death Kaa together with the soul leaves the perishing body. That is why the wise can meet the great transition between the worlds in the full and clear consciousness. Therefore a mixture of seven oils is necessary, because the body does not decompose until Kaa helps a person to be in full consciousness. This condition, as he had been taught, usually lasts no more than for three days for beginners. Those with more experience could often stay in it for forty days, but longer was impossible, because the mixture dissolved in the body and ceased to act. And if someone did not want to return back to the Earth or forgot the way to it, his body would die. Horus was just watching his thoughts and felt that even the smell of incense, which smoked in small vessels on the chains in the hands of the priests, also pleasantly invigorated and helped to see everything clearly. He remembered the teachings of Toth, the great in the three worlds, and realized that now he finally became fully aware of their deep meaning: 'You would separate earth from fire, the subtle from the gross, carefully and with great skill...'

The priests indeed were very proficient. Everything was happening so quickly and easily that the soul has experienced a strong and undisturbed joy. And what awaited him was explained in the instruction that followed immediately after the former:

'This entity ascends from earth to sky and then descends again to the ground, perceiving the power of higher and lower regions of the world.'

Finally, all the corridors and lifts were passed. His body was placed in a large granite sarcophagus. Priests chanted last prayers and giving him a slight bow with a nod, turned and left. His wrapped body was lying in the coffin, and he was floating in the chamber looking around, wondering what to do next. There were no patterns or inscriptions on smooth and clean walls, perhaps not to distract. The only things that could attract the attention were two rectangular holes in the opposite walls. As soon as he thought that he needed to look at them, at that very moment he found that with a half of his invisible body he was inside one of them. Horus saw a bluish and soft light flowing along the stone path from a distant star, and then he remembered the words of his teachers told a day before: 'A ray of a star is a path for the soul.' So, does it mean he has to go on this path? No sooner he thought about it, then he saw himself flying inside the pyramid. A few moments after he flew out of it like an arrow, very easily and quickly he went into the night sky. He recalled his old astonishment in his childhood when for the first time he was left one-to-one with the starry sky and he again saw that it extended infinitely in depth and it seemed a huge, vast and densely populated grand valley. But this time there was a significant difference — there were much more stars. The stars almost completely filled the whole infinitude that opened to the eyes, and what delighted him the most was that he could hear their voices much clearer than in the childhood. These voices were like soft and gentle sounds of distant bells, but the amazing charm was that their sounds were wonderful and unheard-of melodies. To his profound amazement he could understand what they were saying to each other. However, he understood it quite relatively and peculiar, and he would not even try to translate this conversation of stars in human language, because he could find nothing that was even vaguely similar.

How can one express the inexpressible? What words can describe immense and indescribable? We are all brothers, my dear friends, how happy our meeting is — all these simple and clear formulas did not reflect even a thousandth of what was happening in the cosmos. Why, then, it seemed to him that he understood the voices of stars? Yet he certainly understood them, although he would not be able to explain or translate them to anyone. Each and every chime, even the most quiet and distant, light as a breeze and gentle as wondrous fragrance of a flower, echoed in him and sounded within himself as he felt it. He felt becoming one with the boundless Universe. Horus knew that all this greatness, to which he is now inextricably linked, lives and exists not only outside but inside of him. And then the wise words of the great Toth finally became clear to him: 'The universe is a circle in which the center is everywhere and the circumference is nowhere' and 'Small is similar to great, and what is on the top is similar to what is below to fulfill the miracle of unity.' Once Hept-Saft, the Grand Hierophant of Egypt, wisely explained to him in earthly words the law of the One. Yet, Horus realized this great truth only now, when he experienced it, or rather he has become everything and realized that everything is in him, and he is in everything. He wanted to hug all this boundless world, he wanted to do something great and incredibly beautiful to feel that he was worthy of such great honor — to be a part of Him...

The entire Universe unfolded before his immaterial eyes. He moved, swam, flew faster than a meteor passing by colored stars that could be seen from all sides like clusters on the branches of the infinite and incredibly delightful garden. Sometimes he stopped and gazed at them. Then he saw planets that revolved around stars and with their voices they also participated in a grand dance of the cosmos. Horus gazed at those spheres that did not shine as bright as star which were flaming and bristling with rays in all directions. The planets shone with reflected light coming from their mothers, the suns. And when his attention was focused on them, in his mind's eye appeared something like a page of a book where he saw all that existed on this planet. He saw countless species of living creatures: wild and domesticated, floating in the water and flying in the air, running on the land and swarming on it. They were of all sizes conceivable and inconceivable, from huge to very tiny and almost imperceptible, with the incredible variety of forms, sometimes similar to something more or less familiar, but often not amenable to any comparison with what he ever saw. It was enough for him to transfer the focus from one planet to another, when instantly another page of the book appeared in his mind. And again he saw myriads of living beings, whose life was incomprehensible for him. Sometimes he saw creatures entirely different by kind and type, and he immediately realized that they possessed intelligence. He saw the boundless horizons of their planets that were covered with bizarre and beautiful buildings. Horus knew that they were inhabited by people, even though the appearance of these creatures was often very different from the sentient inhabitants of his native Earth.

At one of these planets Horus tried to discern a great city but failing to find its edges finally realized that the entire planet has been built up with houses and buildings with regular intervals between them. Buildings were not only on the land but on the seas as well. When the shore ended, the buildings continued down the surface of the crystal clear emerald turquoise water. He noticed that they were under the water, too. On other planets there were other intelligent beings and other cities, often as endless and covering the entire surface and sometimes even a significant space above the surface in the air. Horus saw many vimanas, but they were very different from ones familiar to him on the Earth in size, color, altitude. Again the most importantly they infinitely varied in forms, and he sometimes could compare them with some bird or insect and sometimes with none of it at all. Some planets had big seas and oceans, while others had more land. Sometimes the sea and water were quite small and insignificant. And everywhere we lived hosts, myriads and myriads of living beings.

THE HEIRS OF ATLANTIS AND WISE MEN OF EGYPT

Sometimes, when his attention was focused on some of them, especially on those who were intelligent, they, too, noticed it, and he could silently communicate with them. He needed neither words nor sounds for that. It was enough for him to create some thought and he was immediately understood and at once they gave another thought in response, which was a continuation of his own. After talking for a while with some of them, he thanked them just with a sense of gratitude and having received in response the same appreciation for the communication he went on to examine and explore the infinite Universe. At some point, he found himself thinking that he takes himself as a boy. When he was a kid, his parents used to take him with them. When he came to a new place he used to run there in the garden or yard trying to explore all of its corners. In such cases his mother usually followed him to bring him back. When he grew up he understood that this was due to caution: in the grass or bushes there could be snakes and other animals, dangerous for children. And what dangers can be here now in this boundless and incredible world that is now opened for him? He thought about his parents and questioned himself who he can talk about everything he has seen when he gets back. Will they understand it? Does he have a right to talk or is it also a secret even to the closest? His grandfather would certainly have understood everything, but what about his parents? For a moment in his memory raised those questions that he had been pondering about all his life in case he got a chance to meet the great sages or even the gods themselves. But what can he ask now when the whole universe is opened like a bottomless book? The whole idea of infinite and unlimited opened for him in all its grandiose meaning. He did not look for an answer to these questions and his old questions and soon he was re-absorbed in a large and beautiful star system, which he was rapidly approaching to and which he again began to explore...

Horus lost all sense of time. He forgot all about his body and did not even wonder how many days had passed. Maybe his body had died and decayed completely. He experienced an unprecedented ecstasy and understood that all his previous enthusiasm was only a faint forerunner of all this greatness. After some time which was impossible to measure with any measures of the Earth he used to this striking state and tried to meditate again. And then he again recalled the recent words of his teachers: 'If you can get to know the One, then you will be able to help those who at the bottom.'

25. Compassion

Only now after all the immeasurable time that Horus spent here he became thoughtful and he could not figure out who was there at the bottom and in fact where the bottom was? Maybe the bottom is on the Earth, but where it is in the infinite and joyous space? He tried to remember the Earth and saw that it was really somewhere far away in the direction where his legs should have been. But, oddly enough, he had no legs. In their place there was a soft bluish light, resembling the light of some stars. But the earth seems to become visible, although in its distant darkness it was impossible to see anything. Continuing to blissfully fly among the stars he tried to focus on distant and foreign land and wondered who he could help?

And then Horus heard a vague noise that grew slowly and was approaching. He could not figure out where the noise was coming from, but after some time he heard the faint cry of a baby. Who was this child, Horus thought, and why was he crying? It was the same darkness bellow and the same resounding and distant sound. Horus did not see the crying child and did not know why he was crying, but the joy and inspiration that he felt so strongly came in an unexpected strong contrast with this unknown pain of the other. He wanted to sooth the crying child, to take him in his arms. As he always did in such cases he said: 'What's up, baby? Why are you crying?'

Horus only had time to see that the rumble became stronger, and he found himself in the very thick of it in the depths of the distant darkness, but then he saw the poor man's hut. Then he realized that although he was outside he could see clearly through the walls of woven reed. He saw a young black woman. She was lying on a mat spread upon the earthen floor. She was facing the wall and cried quietly. And then he saw the child who was standing in front of her but somehow he stood outside as if he was kicked out of the house. The child was tired of crying and was just sobbing quietly. The child was very small; Horus tried to discern him and was surprised to see that he was still a newborn baby. Then suddenly it dawned on Horus and he immediately understood — it was the boy who was to be born today, but died during childbirth. His little body was already committed to the earth, and a woman lying on a mat was his mother. She feels the presence of her unfortunate son's soul standing next to her, and it made her crying inconsolably. Horus felt sorry for both of them. The inescapable joy that rang inside of him did not allow him to recognize the insurmountable obstacles. It was bursting out and imperiously demanded to be shared. Horus came up closely to the child and said to him: 'Come on, I'll show you how nice it is to be in the sky!'

The kid did not react to his words and continued to sob quietly. Then, saying nothing more, Horus took the baby in his arms and quickly soared into the sky. He just turned his prayer to the Highest: 'Lord of Osiris! Lead my way in Amenti!'

Almost immediately he heard a silent voice inside: 'It is not the time for children to go to Amenti. Other place is meant for them.'

No sooner Horus understood the meaning of these words, when he saw himself with a child in his hands in a remarkably beautiful garden full of huge strange flowers, bright colored and unusually huge fruits, happily singing birds and children who were everywhere. There were almost adult children and babies as well. They freely played in the field of a whole garden. They splashed in small ponds and streams, leaped from branchy green trees and flew through the air racing with each other. The most daring and frolic of them flew up sharply in the air and, as if teasing others, called to follow them. Horus quietly sat down on the grass and looked at the baby. The baby stopped crying and now was asleep quietly and serenely. Horus stared at his cute and plump face until the child woke up, yawned and began to look around.

'Look, and you also can do like this,' Horus whispered to the baby and soared high with him following after the most playful child. Then he pulled down again and almost immediately they were surrounded by a crowd of very small children, who did not dare to fly so high but saw in Horus hands a new member of their jolly community.

Runaround of smiling faces quickly whirled around them, sometimes approaching them very close, sometimes quickly moving away until finally the awakened baby let out a cry of joy, full of eagerness to plunge into the joint game, and flew out of the Horus hands. Horus just smiled watching them whirling around himself. He was looking at their half-open mouths that were laughing either silently or loudly. He thought how awful it would be for a child to stand there in the dark and cry instead of being part of the bustling combined happiness. He was about to leave this place and go away when the kid broke out of the circle, flew to him and loudly kissed him on the cheek. Then he flew back a little, again turned to him, waved with his little hand and then plunged into the vortex of unstoppable fun...

'How nice that children have their own world,' Horus thought and remembered the old adage: 'Even those who are far from the stars find joy if they are pure.' He began to realize that ordinary people get at least a small portion of goodness from the boundless universal ocean. Then he remembered the child's mother, who also suffered somewhere down there, and again he heard the distant cry mixed with heavy groans. This time it seemed to him that the voice was somewhat different, and when he focused on the one to whom it belonged, he saw a little wider hut and a loudly sobbing woman who was shaking his head from side to side walking around the hut. Horus tried to look at those inside. He saw an old man and an old lady with their adult sons and daughters sleeping on the floor in the middle. A young woman was lying by the wall embracing her baby as small as the one with whom he recently played. Then he noticed that the weeping woman was turning around this very child. And again Horus somehow came to a clear understanding that this baby was born today, too, but his mother died in childbirth from loss of blood. It is she or rather her lonely soul who is now circling and tossing around her child and another woman, who has taken over the role of a mother, the sister of her husband, whose children have already grown up a bit, and she already stopped feeding them with her milk. Horus decided to speak to the unfortunate soul. He came up and said:

'Why to cry in vain sister? Let's go and gather flowers for your boy. When he wakes up, he will inhale their scent and will rejoice.'

The woman fell to her knees: 'Forgive me, o lord Osiris, but I do not want to leave my son...'

Horus was amazed and said innocently: 'I'm not Osiris, sister, but just a humble admirer of him, the same as you. But together we can find a way to him.'

The woman, still with folded hands, humbly said: 'That means you are the radiant son of the lord Osiris. I beg you not to separate me from my boy... Give him back to me...'

And she began to sob again. Horus was taken aback a little. He then collected his thoughts and said: 'Have you not heard the saying 'All, who love and who are separated, meet in Amenti'? If you want I can take you there, and you will find your child there.'

She humbly bowed her head again and he took her hand and in a few moments they found themselves in a huge garden, which was like the ocean to the horizon. Its wide paths resembled streets and were completely sank into the fragrant flowers and flowering trees, which seem to be brightly lit or rather they emit a gentle and colorful light strikingly contrasting with the darkening deep ultramarine sky in the distance. The woman looked around in surprise. She gradually stopped crying and after a while even started to smile slightly. Horus moved easily, leading her by hand and watching her. Then his attention was attracted by the color of the sky. From childhood he liked this color more than any other and its very depth and expressive tone always reminded him of something inexpressibly beautiful and high. This is the color of the sky in the higher worlds...

When Horus looked back at the woman, she was smiling happily and in her hands she carried the baby, who was left at the bottom and who was now sleeping peacefully. Again she knelt in front of Horus and humbly thanked for the great comfort he brought to her. Then she wanted to kiss his hand. He did not expect it and did not have time to stop her. But when he realized that for her the highest world was not a terrible anguish anymore but a new happy home, he said goodbye to her and again went up to the stars...

It took a lot of time; he again descended down and helped those who he had never even seen before. He helped a young soldier, who died defending villagers from bandits, to find a way to Amenti. Warrior also took him for Osiris, and when Horus objected to such too exalted tittle of God undeserved by him, then the soldier began to call him the son of Osiris. Thereafter he helped other man, who previously was seriously ill and even after the great transition in the other world he still wanted to stay in bed which he got very much used to. Horus told him that if he went with him he would finally recover. The man agreed; the desire to become healthy again overcame his habit for disease. Then Horus helped some old woman who did not want to leave her children and grandchildren. He said that the bodies of her loved ones lay on the ground and did not answer her because they themselves are far away, but she could still see them if she came out from the walls of her house. The old woman did not want to move away from her habitual place, but then she believed him and saw the souls dear to her heart. She could again to talk to them as before. Then there was someone else...

He only remembered that the last one was an old man who wanted to see God. And Horus helped him to elevate to the stars. The old man experienced an intense delight and at once became younger, but then after a while, as if unable to bear this joy for long he fell asleep and began to gradually go down to the Earth. Horus went down with him, and then suddenly in his mind emerged what his mentors told him right before he was about to be swaddled, 'If you will attain mastery in this great art, you will be able to save seven souls from suffering. But once you help a seventh, then it will be time to come back...'

26. The Return Point

He remembered the song his mother used to sing over his cradle when he was little. This song had simply and naive words, but they touched him deeply: 'When you came to this world, it was night on the Earth, but the land did not sleep.' He went down gradually as, perhaps, a cautious pilot lowers his vimana when it is dark and he cannot see anything. Horus saw the horizon, saw the reflection of the moon on the waves of the river, and then he remembered that it was that very night when people of celebrate the festival of Mother, the great goddess Mother. They kindle the lights at night in temples, bring them to their homes and set sail them in small canoes on the river. No sooner had he recalled it when he saw thousands of points of light floating down in the darkness among the reflections of the moon. And then he thought of his mother who first met him in this life, who led him to this world. He was surprised to see that his feelings have changed, he was imagining his mother in another way: she started to look like, both externally and internally, one of the image of the goddess Isis that he knew for a long time.

Asmini brought a small burning lamp, lit by fire from the altar in the temple of Isis. She put it on the table and gazed thoughtfully into the distance. She could not sleep and felt very anxious. Her husband woke up, got up, walked over to her and asked: 'Why are you awake, dear?'

'I cannot, my dear,' she said. 'Something is happening to Gorik.'

'What can happen to him?' Rame replied. 'He is already

an adult and he is in the hands of the wisest people of Egypt. Why worry about him?'

'I do not know', said Asmin. 'I do not know, I think so. It's better to ask father.'

Together they went into the next room. Ra-Ta also did not sleep. He was sitting with his scrolls and was writing something. When the daughter came, the old man turned to her and immediately caught her mood.

'Why did you worry, my daughter?' asked the old man.

'Yes, I'm very worried, father, about Gorik. I think he is in pain and in difficulty...'

Ra-Ta thought and then replied: 'Do not worry, dear, he will stand it.'

'Is it so scary, father?'

'It's scary for the timid, Asmik, but our Gorik is not like that.'

'But it may damage his soul?' Asmin asked.

'No, I don't think so. A weak will break, but a weak cannot reach this stage. He's strong, he is already an adult.'

'But why? Why do they torture him? After all, priests are good people, they're not cruel, although they always look stern...'

'What are you saying, daughter? He is not tormented by the priests... He's just returning. Those who had felt the boundless freedom and joy of liberated spirit, return into the body and feel that the whole world becomes their prison cell which presses and does not allow them to breathe; it is difficult and painful at first, but then it goes away.'

She wiped her involuntary tears, bowed to his father and clung to his face:

'So this is the price for wisdom... That is you pay for it with your suffering...

He stroked her hair: 'You have to pay for everything, my daughter... Everything in the manifest world has a downside. The higher the knowledge, the more expensive it is. But it's like meeting after a separation. The bitter parting, the happier the meeting...'

Horus was carried on a stretcher. His body was unwrapped, rubbed and warmed, but the carriers and a few of priests were now silent and did not sing any of prayers and incantations. His mind was not so clear anymore as it was there above. He only remembered that at the end of his smooth descent he saw the great pyramid and realized that he had to go back to the body. He immediately found the sarcophagus chamber, slid with his feet first into his head and returned back to the body. And then everything was like in the fog... His thoughts got mixed, and like any other thinking person, he was trying to understand what was happening to him. It was hard to move even with a hand. The body was shivering and disobeyed. He felt as if thousands of tiny invisible needles tingle him from the tips of the toes to the top of the head. It was something like numbness of the hands and feet when they have been in an awkward position or were exhausted. But he never experienced it simultaneously in the whole body from top to bottom. However, he was told in advance that it would be very difficult after the return, but he should not be scary, because it would soon go away. But the most unpleasant was not this. He tried to focus on his thoughts and was terrified with their crowd...

'What is happening to me?' swept in his mind. 'I was a boundless sky, I was a sweeping wind, I heard the voices of stars, I gave mercy, seeing the suffering... and now I have turned into a weak-willed and crumpled lump of dirt... How horrible! Oh great gods! Why is the destiny of man so cruel?! Why is it so hard to be on earth?!'.

Horus tried to answer to his anxieties. But his thoughts did not heed his own arguments. And the worst thing was that along with the body senses also did not obey him. They inflamed more and more by these strange disturbing thoughts. It was like a complete madness...

27. The Messenger of the Gods

He was put on a bed in an empty room. Then all the priests with their right fingers touched his chest and said: 'Fight, brother!' and left. Horus could not understand what was happening to him. He turned to one side but within him some part of his being moved in the opposite direction. Everything went wrong and came out of the usual control by consciousness. The riven and stabbing pain throughout the body, horror and longing inexpressible by any words and boundless as space. All this burned him inside and out. He clenched his lips with his teeth to the blood. He struggled trying not to scream and cry. But he hardly could do that. His barely muffled moans were bursting out from his very heart and he could not hold them. His eyes were wet, he rubbed them, but to no avail. Sometimes a huge wave of bottomless despair and heartache covered him in such a way that he bit his pillow so as not to scream; he tore his clothes, which seemed, too, burned his body with the vehement fire. The night seemed endless. The room was semi-dark, lit by weak light of lamps. A few times Horus struggled to get up and realized with horror that he could not do even this. The body was not responding to his commands and was making some strange and absurd movements.

Nothing helped, neither appeals to the gods, nor prayers, nor sacred syllables of spells, nothing could stop this never-ending nightmare. Tired of fighting with this terrible condition Horus simply lay and quietly and helplessly sobbed like a baby, who he took with him to the abode of children. He remembered this child and thought that it was good that he could help the poor kid. Maybe now someone would be able to help him. Why are all gone, and no one comes to him? And yet, something was slowly changing around him. The dawn already blazing somewhere far began to penetrate with its pale rays into the small windows near the ceiling, and the darkness in the room gradually decreased. He looked at his clothes and saw that it was all torn and turned into rags. He was very sorry for what he did with the clothes his beloved mother made with much labor: at first she made spun yarn, then weaved the fabric from it, and then sew beautiful and elegant tunic for him. But as it became lighter in the room, he noticed with surprise that it was not at all something his mom worked for weeks on. The color was very different, much darker, and the fine patterns were not seen, too. Horus realized at last that wise and prudent priests took care even about his clothes. Knowing in advance what awaited him after his return they dressed him in something more rough. Horus thanked them from the bottom of his confused and restless heart and called them blessed. The room became almost completely lighted, and Horus tried to examine it a bit turning his disobedient body with difficulty. Soon, to his profound amazement he saw a chair on the ground not far from himself. A man sat in it. It was all blurred in Horus eyes. He could not see properly, but somehow instinctively understood that it was a stranger, and not from the local priests and Hierophants. Horus blew through quivering lips: 'Who are you?'

The stranger's face was absolutely still like of a stone statue, but in a clear and firm glance of brown eyes there were high thoughts, the greatness of strength and a calm and wise compassion. He did not open his mouth, but Horus heard his voice as if in his mind: 'I'm here to answer your questions.'

Horus still could not collect his thoughts properly, but he asked a question that tormented him the most: 'What is happening to me? Why is it so heavy?'

The answer did not come immediately, and it was like a flash of soft and saving light: 'It is always not easy to get back from the higher worlds in the matter. It is especially hard for those who are just born. Therefore babies usually cry. Now you feel something similar. Besides, you stayed for a long time and you did not want to come back. Usually one starts with three days, then take it to forty. One should begin with nearest worlds, and then rise to the top ones. In this way there will be less suffering. But you immediately rushed to the very highest abode and stayed there for forty-two days. That's why your body hurts so strongly and your spirit is experiencing great anguish, but it will soon pass.

Horus was surprised with such a simple and wise explanation and noticed that he felt better. Then he began to think of the places in sacred books. Probably the stranger helped him with this also. The books described that the gods themselves have been to the Earth in human form and endured all the hardships of earthly life with full consciousness and great dignity. Horus asked: 'Even the gods passed all the tests and initiations as we, mere mortals?'

The answer came in the form of thought: 'From the very first and the lower stage up to infinity. The intelligence must learn to curb the chaos first in himself in order to create from it in the outside world.'

'So, this is the meaning of life on Earth?'

'Yes, to come closer to the Mind of stars whose voices you heard and understood.'

In his head Horus heard a passage from some book whose name he could not remember, maybe because it was one of those books which he had never seen in the temple libraries, but sometimes he read them in his dreams, when some high and bright unearthly creatures showed him the unearthly manuscripts. Perhaps, the sage sitting on a chair helped him with this. He saw before himself gold shining letters as hanging in the air: 'To go through countless ages to become the same as the Mind of stars and to understand the Mind that created the stars — to become one with Wisdom of the One'.

Horus was again surprised by the depth and gigantic scope of the stranger's thought. This he had not seen even among the greatest sages known to him. He imagined the endless steps of a stair leading to the boundless distances of Cosmos, where yesterday he was so happy and easy to be. Then he tried to watch himself from a side and realized that something was happening with his feelings. They could be compared with a spoiled child, who had been loved, caressed and made happy and who was accustomed to rejoice. And then this child suddenly would end up in the dark during a sandstorm, and he was left alone by everyone to suffer hopelessly and restlessly wander. That's why he was actually worried. This contrast was quite unusual and only intensified the feeling of horror. But feelings should submit to ideas; they are only their effect. It was enough to realize this clearly and almost all his burden was gone. And again when the daylight came he was surprised to see that the stranger, who was sitting on a chair, disappeared...

Horus experienced this new astonishment, but then, ceasing to strain and to rise from his bed, he leaned wearily on his hard bed and for the first time finally he immersed in sleep...

When he awoke, the sun was already high and began to move toward the sunset. Horus tried to get up, and he did. He saw a beautiful coat, stitched by his mother. It lay in his feet as before. Horus put it on after taking off somebody else's clothes, torn by him in rags for all this infinitely long and unbearably heavy night. Once again he mentally thanked the priests for wisdom and kindness. Then he walked out of the room, slightly staggering. There was no one in the spacious room of the temple. In the next room, smaller in size, there was only a lonely old priest standing by the door and looking out. Horus noted that his mind was finally awakened and he started to think about this old man and estimate his condition: if he is the priest then he has passed the first small initiations, but since he has no signs of the high ranks of clergy, it means he has still not gotten the great initiations. Horus stopped the flow of his thoughts, and said to himself: if this person belongs to the spiritual he has to withstand all the burden of staying in the corporeal world, realizing the inevitability of it all. Then he walked over to the old man, humbly greeted him, bowed before him and kissed his hand. The elder replied with a nod and silently blessed Horus with a hand gesture. Horus went outside and felt the warmth of the sun. The heat has already decreased and the rays of the majestic luminary were very pleasing pleasant for the body. He walked slowly and intently, looking around as if trying to remember how this usual and familiar from childhood world looks like. Sunset was just beginning when he got home.

A someone's chariot stood in the courtyard. As soon as he came to the stairs he saw Asmini. She came out sensing that he was coming and silently hugged him. Then came the father and grandfather, and for the first time Horus saw a special smile on grandfather's face. He wasn't just proud of his grandson, but it seemed he foresaw all this and had no doubt that Horus would win and survive. Ra-Ta paternally kissed him as well as his daughter and his son-in-law. Then together they walked into the home of abandoned guest. It was an officer, the messenger of the Pharaoh. But this time the king called not the father of Horus but the grandfather.

28. The Mission

Iltar and Wotan reported that the vehicle was ready for take-off. However Ra-Ta asked them to wait. It took another half an hour before his old friend came. Mayum walked quickly, he was covered with dust. He went to the Ra-Ta and handed him a small wooden object.

'Here, my brother Ra-Ta,' he said. 'It is a comb of Afteb's daughter. Find them, my brother. Let the gods help you.'

Mayum hugged him. Then Ra-Ta entered the viman and the ship soared into the sky. Pilots have directed the machine towards the sunset. Horus again looked down and wondered: that time he was still a child, but now he was seeing the Earth from a height for the second time. He watched how cities and villages pass by below. Then he saw the boundless sea with some islands at the horizon.

The stars have already appeared in the sky, but their machine as if overtaking the movement of the Earth was always in front of a setting sun.

Horus even thought that at the end of the travel, which lasted several hours and was a little longer than when they were flying to get their grandfather back, the sun was even higher as if before sunset. He was still not sleepy, and while Ra-Ta was talking to the pilots, Horus was looking down intently at the islands floating by, lonely in a vast array of the sea. Soon the big land appeared on the horizon.

Answering the questions of the elder the pilots talked about vimanas which receive Mash-Mac not from the air from the tower but use special liquid created for this purpose. If their island is flooded such vehicles can fly for some time, but then it will be necessary to make the special liquid again, because its supply will exhaust together with the power of crystals.

Viman began to descend. Horus watched with interest and thought to himself: 'Is this really the country of Aztlan?' he had heard so much about it, and finally he can see it with his own eyes.

Viman flew low and smoothly over the fields and canals, over the beautiful buildings. Horus could see from above how they were decorated and how gems glittered in them. He looked surprised and realized that he had never seen anything of the kind.

After a while, when Viman has gone down enough, they were above the center of a big city, surrounded on all sides by several circles of water. The air was filled with fluff from trees.

The viman landed, they got out and saw around the large and beautiful buildings. They have been waited for. Among those who met them was Las-lu, the governor of the Sas city, and councilors of the emperor Alta and senior priests.

The guests were welcomed and accommodated in one of these big and beautiful buildings that proved to be specially built for visitors. The building inside was also nice and had all the amenities.

Horus could not sleep most of the night; he was agitated with novelty and uncommonness of this place. Actually it was the first large and long journey in his life. But these feelings were added also with those that he experienced before during sleepless nights: when he felt the presence of the invisible and powerful beings, and it filled his soul with light and power, inspired and nourished it, allowing it to grow and become stronger. His mind sometimes compared it with the way his mother had watered the plants in the garden, and he thought that the celestial goddess-mistress similarly watered her crops in the garden of life — the souls and consciousness of people. This all started to happen with Horus after the great test. Probably, the dark red drink which he drunk from the cup filled by the great Hierophant, contributed to this. The drink itself had a pleasant taste and vaguely resembled a wine that Horus tried several times already during his young life. But its impact was incomparable; it did not pass the next day but remained for a long time, maybe even forever.

It was also distinguished by the fact that it not only elevated the mood but seemed to sharpen and intensify feelings, not all, but only those that according to him and the sages were the highest and holy. The ability to understand the unknown and to penetrate into the invisible also increased. Besides, there were fresher and unexpected manifestations associated with how or rather whom he himself felt. Then there were sometimes really amazing things. Often, when he as trying to fall asleep, tossing and turning around, he began to feel that his teeth in his mouth seemed to have changed, he felt they became large and even huge. The same thing could happen with other parts of his body, most often it manifested in his arms. It seemed that his hands would become several times larger and more powerful, they appeared huge and could possibly do anything he liked, even to uproot trees or reach to the stars. In such moments Horus remembered as older people joked about those who were too arrogant; they said they usually felt themselves elephants. May be this irony could be applied to him? But he still did not understand what it all might mean. One day he decided to ask about this from the Ra-Ta and got a simple and wise answer from him: it's all very good and means that the power and the soul of a person grow. As it used to be in such cases, here at Poseidonis he could not fall asleep more than half of the first night and only when it was not long before the Dawn he went to sleep.

29. The Alta

The next morning Horus cheerfully without feeling any fatigue after a half-sleepless night went to the main repository of books together with his grandfather and his friends Iltar and Wotan. This building was not so big and also not very high. But as later he saw, the building had a lot of underground floors, it went deep into the ground, but he could not say how many stories were there. They searched floor by floor. On each story there were piles of ancient scrolls and books of various kinds, made from different materials and written in different languages. The keepers of this great library helped them to select the main and most important books that were to be saved in the first place. Their content covered such fields of human knowledge as the history of races and peoples, geography, medical art, philosophy, mathematics, astronomy and other sciences as well as literature. The guests were learning a lot to their surprise, it turned out that the country of Aztlan used to be much bigger once and had undergone changes and floods. Her first capital was the city of the Golden Gate. It was flooded many thousands of years ago. Twice there were large migrations when it grew very cold. Everything was covered with ice and people had to migrate to warmer places. However, both times it was temporary, and many descendants of the migrants used to return and settle in their country again. There were books about those peoples who originated on the island very long time ago. Under the leadership of their leaders they moved and settled in other countries. Horus learned that the inhabitants of a distant country such as the Gobi also mostly came from Aztlan, but it was a long time ago, even before the great flood.

In addition to books Horus saw also other things: he saw the sculptures. Sometimes he asked to explain what this or that sculpture illustrated. Sometimes he saw the bas-reliefs. Here and there he saw animated maps with real water and real plants. As he was told it was the descriptions of what such and such country looked like in such and such times; or it was a picture of events that took place here. Not only in books but on the walls he saw pictures and drawings of various strange animals he had never met. He was explained what were these animals, what were their habits when they lived and who they turn to later.

They visited floor by floor, collecting the most valuable from the treasure that has been accumulated here over the centuries, but they had not reached the bottom. But newer and newer questions were running through Horus's mind. Once he stopped at the sculptural group which featured seven people. It was interesting that these statues were of completely different sizes: one was very small, the one that stood in the center and a little closer to the right side; and those which were at the edges were huge, they were several times bigger. Horus said: 'What is it?'

Library staff looked at each other and said nothing. Seeing that they do not speak, Ra-Ta went on to explain: 'This is what people used to look like before,' he said and pointed to the highest statue at the edges. 'Then they became this,' he pointed to a second statue at each end. 'And then this. And then they reduced to this size here' and he pointed to the smallest statue in the center.

Horus was surprised. He already knew that the people of Aztlan were a head taller all the rest. But he did not know they used to be so big. 'But why does nature reduce the height of the human?' Horus asked.

Residents of Aztlan were silent again, and once more Ra-Ta said for them:
'Because a true greatness, dear Horus, is not in height

or in the power of the hands or feet. True greatness is in the soul and mind. And when people understand it: that they should primarily rely on their mind rather than bestial force, then their mother nature will return them their former strength, but it will be in harmony with their new mind.

30. The Priestess

Every day they came back to the library and learned a lot. Horus was always joyful. Even his grandfather was inspired by seeing every time so many new "colors of wisdom" around, as he called books. But Horus had other reason for the excitement and anticipation — Una. That time in their home Una spent with her parents only three weeks. Helping his father and mother she was all the time with them, and they all used to come back by the evening when Horus returned from the temple. The young people were reserved to talk in the presence of adults, but Horus felt that at the meeting she smiled as sincerely, though restrained, as he. It was already many years since the guests completing their task given by the governor of Alta, returned to their country. That time they said only a few words about their mission. It was connected with the preservation and future placement of countless books of Aztlan. And now Horus and Ra-Ta came to them with the same purpose. Horus was confident he would see Una. And he was not mistaken, it happened on the third day. But it was only momentary and to his distress now they worked separately. However, sometimes Una or her parents met him and his grandfather on one of the floors of the large library. However Horus did not know where he could find them.

Now, as before, when Horus saw the girl for the first time, her image was constantly before his eyes. Some strange things were happening with him. At first he could not understand what it meant. It happened every time when he and his grandfather went for a walk, whether it was day or night, or even at night when the streets were illuminated with night lights. Each time when they went out to walk, when a woman appeared in the street Horus saw Una in her and was about to joyfully come up to her and say hello. But when he moved forward and approached her closer, he suddenly began to understand that something strange was happening to him and each time he found himself in an awkward position. Having come close enough when he was going to talk to her, he was suddenly surprised to see that it was not Una but some other girl. It confused him.

This happened not once or twice, it constantly repeated, and Horus did not understand what was happening to him. When he saw another woman and took her for Una, he was sure it was her. But as soon as he approached her, this illusion would vanish and he saw that it was a completely different person. Sometimes the lady was totally different in height, hair color, clothing and age. Occasionally, for some reason he mistook a little girl for Una or, vice versa, an adult woman. Then he asked himself: is it not silly?

Then, thinking about what was happening to him, Horus came to the most simple and logical conclusion for a reasonable person. He said to himself: 'If you always see her everywhere, it means she is in you.' He realized that he saw her in his mind.

It went like that until one day he once again saw a young woman on the street and took her for Una. But this time he did not direct his steps toward her, but instead pulled himself, saying: 'This is not her, go quietly.' And he was calm as long as he thought like this, but when he caught up with her, he noticed that the girl had the same bangle as that of Una.

He had already learned not to pay attention to the fact that the faces of all the women seemed to him like her. But now, seeing the bracelet on her arm, he looked up and saw that it was really Una. He thought, 'What a wonderful life! When you are wrong it seems that you are right, but when you're right, you think you're wrong.'

Then, seeing a smile on Una's face, he joyfully greeted her and asked about what she did and when she would come back to the library to help them in collecting the legacy of the wise men of her country. Una said she was just going there.

Reluctantly Horus made an effort to say that he was going to a very different place sent by his grandfather. In any case, he firmly promised to return soon for the joint work of book selection.

He had quickly executed the order of Ra-Ta and upon his way back he felt as if wings appeared behind his back to help him to return sooner. Again he saw Una in his mind's eye but this time she was smiling and he, not yet seeing her physically, was smiling back at her. Back at the library, Horus at once quickly and unerringly found her in one of the many floors. Under the guidance of Ra-Ta and senior priests they have quickly and happily completed their work of collecting the scrolls. They lifted them up to the room with the most important books, subjected to be rescued and exported in the first place. Even there Ra-Ta went on to examine them. He even quickly went through some of them. Despite his advanced age he had an unquenchable thirst for knowledge, more than an ordinary young student. Horus and Una came out so that not to disturb him. They situated on the balcony of the building, framed with beautiful columns with the stucco mouldings in the form of flowers and plants. The day ended, the sun was going to set, they looked happily into each other's eyes or in the distance, talking about different matters, about their parents, a little about their countries and about the future relocation. Horus then withstood a brief pause as if to collect his thoughts and asked Una: 'You are so beautiful and intelligent... I've never seen such a beautiful girl like you... Tell me, did you ever think that in the future you would have daughter and son as beautiful and clever as you?'

Una looked away and then said as if to herself: 'When I was small, my mom asked our wise elder priestess Ree to see my future...'

Horus inadvertently stopped breathing, she continued: 'She said that when I grow up, I'll be a priestess like my father and mother, but I will have my family and children not here on our island but in another distant country... And there I will meet someone who is destined for me by fate and the gods...'

Then she turned back to Horus. He saw in her eyes a complete and infinite trust and it was so sincere that he felt uncomfortable at the very thought that someone could deceive this trust. Horus recalled what was told by that strange bluish light that flashed somewhere on top of his head on the day when he first saw Una: 'Do not worry, you'll be okay with her.' That moment he immediately believed it, and now he was convinced once again. He understood everything without words, he silently and gently hugged her and tenderly whispered: 'Whoever destined for you in a distant country, having seen you once he would never be able to forget you. He wants you to always be close, he wants to enjoy for life your beautiful face and light in your eyes...'

31. Deliverance

The days passed one after the other, the number of bundles of various books in different languages increased, and finally one evening when the sun had set Iltar said that although not all the books were still collected, but perhaps they already have as much as can go in their vimana. At that moment Ra-Ta thought, then he got out of his travel bag the thing that Mayum gave him before takeoff: 'Now it's time to fly to the city of Peos.'

Horus also wanted to fly with them. 'I'll go with you, too, my grandfather,' he said.

But the old Ra-Ta shook his head: 'No, Horus, you will stay here. If something happens to us, you will carry all the books home.'

Then he kissed his grandson on the cheek and together with Iltar and Wotan they sat in viman. The big bird smoothly took off and disappeared in the dark night sky. They flew not long. The north end of the island was not very far away. Soon their devices began to show the place where the mistress of a wooden comb was. Stopping over the place and having decreased a altitude a little, Iltar said to Wotan: 'It's a big house. Probably, it belongs to one of the rich. The yard is so large that we can land right there.'

Wotan replied: 'The guards are surely there. And even if we find a place, we should take care of our safty.'

'Do not worry,' Iltar said, referring to Ra-Ta, 'We will be able to neutralize the guards.'

Then he pointed to the navigation instruments and continued: 'Here in this corner in this part of the yard there is some sort of a structure. Now, at night they are located there and probably they just sleep.'

'Welcome!' Ra-Ta said. 'Let's go do our duty for the One.'

Viman went down into the yard smoothly without turning the lights on. All three of them came out of it. However, as Iltar anticipated, the guards were really in place. They did not sleep. A few moments later four soldiers of the house-owner surrounded them. Iltar raised his hand with the rod and switched the button from green to red right in front of them. He said calmly but firmly: 'We came by the will of the Alta ruler. You have no right to arrest strangers here. If you try to stop us or even make one wrong move, I'll turn you into ashes!'

The guards were frightened and frozen, they did not have anything with them except clubs. Ra-Ta went to the corner of the yard, that Iltar pointed to. After finding the door in the dark and entering the dark room, where he could not see anything, he said loudly: 'Afteb, where are you? Answer me!'

After a moment he heard a muffled voice from the corner: 'I am here, my lord. Who are you?' 'I've come for you, Afteb! Collect all your children. We're going home.'

Some commotion began in the darkness. Obviously there were a lot of people there. A few seconds later the old head of the family lit a lamp, and it became clear what was happening. All his relatives and descendants, older and younger, woke up and gathered in a crowd around a newcomer. They examined him with surprise but did not dare to ask any questions. Afteb did not seem to believe his own eyes and ears when for the first time after so many years he heard his native language from a stranger. He walked over and asked him in amazement: 'Who are you, sir? You really came for us?' 'Yes, Afteb, I'm a friend of Mayum. He is waiting for you. Come!' briefly said Ra-Ta and moved toward the door.

All members of a big family followed him with unconcealed joy. When they went out into the yard, the Ra-ta noticed a red light on the Wotan's staff; they both kept their weapons ready. None of the guards did dare to move until all twenty three people followed by Ra-Ta got in viman. Finally Iltar told the guards: 'Tell your master that if the troops of Alta ruler came here, he would have paid for his evil. But now we will not touch him. We have liberated the prisoners and it is enough for us. If you dare to stop us or throw at least a stone in our vimana, I will make all your yard and home into the molten crater of the volcano, clear?!' strictly asked Iltar.

The guards were seriously scared. They replied: 'Why, sir, we will not dare, do not worry.' 'Tell your master that sooner or later he will answer for everything.' 'With these words Iltar and Wotan returned to the cabin. Viman quietly and imperceptibly soared into the sky and headed back south to Alta, where Horus waited for them.

During the travel the most of the Afteb's kinsmen had been sitting modestly and quietly and only one elderly person asked Ra-ta about what was happening at home and how it was that the old man came to save them. Ra-Ta briefly told him of all the events that have occurred since the time of their absence. Then Afteb asked: 'Do you know our leader Mayum for a long time?' Ra-Ta smiled. 'We have been friends with him since our youth. And he is like brother to me.' 'Thank you, good sir,' said Afteb, and to this Ra-Ta answered: 'Justice, my brother, is always the will of the gods. And those who serve them must be fair anywhere anytime.'

Viman was slowly landing. The lights below were already seen. The city also did not sleep and life flowed in it. The street lights and the lights inside the houses gave a sense of hidden tension.

All the people of Alta knew what awaited them. Although they would hit the road not tomorrow, but those who did not sleep at this hour thought about their fate, about past and future. The present did not matter any longer.

32. Osiris

All the way home Horus thought about Una. He knew that she also remembers him. Together with her parents she was soon to move to his country, but no one knew for sure when that would happen. Everyone was waiting for the order of the governor of Alta. Iltar and Wotan confidently drove their vimana over the sea and desert. They landed it exactly to where these chronicles were kept. The most number of books should have been brought by the residents of Aztlan, but the most important and valuable ones as the heritage for all mankind were decided to be brought in advance and stored in a special secret rooms under the Sphinx. When the viman got down a large group of priests came up to it. All of them together with those who have just arrived quickly placed the precious cargo in the underground premises. Then the craftsmen-bricklayers began to seal its entrance. Within hours Ra-Ta and Horus were at home. Wotan and Iltar brought them. Then, on the insistent invitation of the owner they went into the house and after having dined with him and others they said warm goodbye to everyone and said that they must urgently return to Alta, because the governor had another important mission.

After bidding farewell to them, Horus retired to his room. He tried to analyze the thoughts that came to him when Iltar and Wotan sat in their Vimana. It seemed to him that they would never meet, at least, in this lifetime. After thinking in this way he came to the conclusion that it may be for the simple reason: now these industrious and responsible people will be sent to some other country far from his native Egypt. Or that because of the imminent flood of Poseidonis vimanas will not fly any longer because the crystal that transmits energy to them through the air will also be flooded or destroyed together with Alta and other cities on the island. The sense of impending huge and irreversible changes, prevailed among the residents of Poseidonis, passed on to him as well. Again he thought of Una and her parents who soon will have to move to them forever. Horus, along with his wise grandfather, belonged to the priestly caste and knew well its rules. Priests are not forbidden to have families. But only those who were married had to follow quite a long period of celibacy before the execution of the most important ceremonies. But there was no use for the married to wait for new and higher initiations. But he did not want to abandon Una, sensing her boundless trust to himself. He was ready, if necessary, even to risk his life, but not to betray the hope and faith of this girl. On the other side Horus did not want to refuse from further knowledge, which was the very meaning of life for him. He was never faced with such a choice; almost all the girls whom he knew and whom he treated as sisters, talked to him about the most ordinary everyday topics. For a young man thirsty for the wisdom all of them were of no interest.

Una was strikingly different not only because of her unearthly beauty, but she also had a profound mind, she could keep the conversation with the most educated people, but sometimes in certain subjects she even shared her knowledge that Horus did not have. Horus understood that his meeting her was a gift of fate for him. He was surprised to discover that Una had passed all six small initiations at her home. He had hardly seen priestesses, though he had heard that a priestess of Isis in his native Egypt had a third great initiation. The same had his own grandfather and holy Hept-Saft: the highest level, which priests called "Torch" or "Lamp". A human could attain such level only with the help of the senior priests. When he first heard this name he immediately appreciated how accurate it was; he remembered the light streaming from the grandfather's eyes. Hept-Saft's eyes emanated the same soft and kind light. Horus knew also about three other great initiations but never heard their names. These levels with their dates and achievements had nothing to do with people. Only gods could decide about them. They used to conduct tests and give new knowledge to those who had stood the trial. Only once did he allow himself to ask Ra-Ta about it, and his wise grandfather answered that the gods watch what a person serves to, how high and transpersonal his purpose and how selfless his service is. He said that the level of "Candle" automatically attracts the attention of the residents of heaven, but it has a lot of different subsequent stages which people do not always have time to pass even for the rest of their life, not to mention the higher initiations, which are no use to discuss.

It was the main thing that inspired Horus. In his natural modesty he would never have dared to even think that he could so quickly get such a high initiation and, being so young, soon grow to the level of the wisest Hept Saft or Ra-Ta. But to progress to it and to devote all his life to it was just what he wanted the most. He has already passed the first two great stages when he passed the test of recognition in the heart and saw Hept-Saft for the first time. Horus did not doubt even for a moment that it was he. After the second stage Horus became convinced how quickly and clearly many of his thoughts began to come true even when externally he did nothing for this sake. People and animals began to understand him, even when he was silent. Sometimes it was enough for him to just cast his glance to make living beings to carry out his mental order. He then realized how wise his teachings was. It helped to clear his thoughts and compelled him to pass new tests, because even if low thoughts are very few, having such power he would have turned into an evil and dangerous sorcerer. After all, as he often heard, there are not only white magicians, but also dark ones.

Horus pondered all night about it and in the morning when he came to the temple he approached his teacher and asked to give him a new and important challenge. The teacher said: 'My brother, we appreciate your dedication and commitment. But do you remember that this trial is followed by an initiation, the greatest one which mortals can get from humans, and that only great Hierophant of Egypt together with the priestess of Isis can give permission for it?

Horus well remembered and understood that: 'Yes, Father, I remember. And I humbly beg to inform the great Hierophant of my request.'

The priest said after a pause: 'Well, brother Horus, I'll tell him of your desire.'

Horus humbly thanked the counselor and entered upon his temple duties of which he got out of habit during his absence.

Three weeks passed. The teacher came up to him and said that the decision about of the trial has already been made and the day was appointed. Horus was overjoyed. He thanked his mentor and proceeded to his usual routine in the temple. Soon came the day of tests. Horus put on the same elegant beautiful chiton stitched by his mother and went back to where he was waited. Before the door closed behind him his teacher said only one sentence: 'Do not stop and do not slow down your steps until you see his holiness.' Horus thanked him and headed for the unknown. A thin strip of light on the floor led him as it had been before. There were no sounds, no voices. He walked pretty fast and after only a few minutes he saw some light at the end of the corridor. A little later, when he came close enough, he began to distinguish the door to which he promptly moved. Then he noticed that the door slightly gleamed, and when he came closer, he realized that it was made of metal, probably of copper or bronze. Only then he thought that the door might be locked. He was told not to slow down, but what would happen then? 'Probably I'll get bump on my forehead,' he thought and remembered the expression 'to break the wall with a forehead.' Such price seemed to him quite insignificant for the highest initiation, but the door was already close and he decided not to stop. When Horus was almost against the door he instinctively reached out but the door would not give in. It was seemed to be locked and he realized it at the very last moment. The only thing he had to do was to slightly turn his head and put his shoulder forward.

The shoulder banged on the door but he still tried to continue to move forward and when he met obstacle with all his body he felt with surprise and then watched as the door gave way. No, it did not open but seemed to disintegrate or broke up in pieces which all together synchronously moved away in different directions. Horus literally burst into the room which was sufficiently lighted. He saw only Hept-Saft there. There was neither the clergy nor the preparations for the ceremony as before, nothing. Just an empty room and two chairs. Folding his arms, he greeted: 'Hail, the holiest!'

'Hail, brother. You've passed the ultimate test of the humans. Then you will be tested by the gods themselves.'

Horus thought for a moment, and then said: 'Your Holiness, I do not feel that know all human wisdom. On the contrary, I know that still do not know much. So much that I'm ready to learn forever.' Hierophant smiled in approve: 'A true knower never thinks he passed all the way. He always considers himself a disciple. But at the same time you must remember that everything is in you, all the secrets and answers.'

Horus was surprised, he understood the meaning of this wisdom, but always considered that the most important is the training and assistance from the more mature and older: 'Inside of me? But I have so many questions and so little knowledge even in comparison to my wise grandfather or you, o holy Hept Saft...'

The elder replied, slowly and majestically: 'When the One becomes all the beings for the seeker who sees the unity, then what ignorance, what sadness can he have? It extends everywhere — bright, bodiless, pure, invulnerable for the evil. The knowing, cognizant, omnipresent and self-existent, it has properly and forever distributed all the things in their places. What does it mean, my brother?'

Horus perfectly remembered those lines together with the continuation and understood the logic of this wisdom: 'It means the One is in all and hence it is also in me. It is me. But is it enough to remember it? What to do with It and and how to serve It?'

'What is left for a human? Here you came to me armed with the Secret, but what can I give you when the final crown is kept in you. Sit down and open the last gates. I will make your ascension easier for you with my last prayer. Ascend to the highest, brother. I will help you.'

They sat down. Horus began to focus. He again felt the Hierophant's help. Again the same familiar powerful light and bright whirlwind caught his spirit and help to ascend to the high sky. After a while he noticed an unusual thing: he could see from the point at which he was and at the same time he saw himself from the outside. At first he did not understand what was happening, but gradually began to notice how streams of radiant light next to him formed a shining beautiful and ethereal image. Horus admiringly looked at it trying to figure out who it was. When the image became clearly distinguishable Horus wanted to cry out "Osiris!", because that's how he imagined God. For some time he was in a strong admiration and could not say anything even to himself. Then, when he came to senses a little, his memory has emerged as his most soul of ordinary people take for Osiris even after his explanation that it is not so, continued to be called the son of Osiris. Maybe he's too confusing? However, Horus noticed another unusual thing: he saw himself from the outside just where there was a glowing silhouette of god. Horus was a bit perplexed. If it is not Osiris himself then where is this god, if his face so clearly shines here? When he thought about it, everything changed. The room had disappeared. He was again somewhere among the stars trying to understand where it was. He heard a voice within him: 'Constellation of Orion.'

The constellation nearby looked very different than when he saw it from far away from Earth. Next to one of the stars he noticed the outline of a ship that resembled a huge vimana or even a floating city with a very complex structure, bordered on all sides with lights of different colors and brightness. Many small bright figures gently circled around it. Horus began to draw to this place and heard an unusual rhythmic music. He had never heard such music, there were a rapid fascinating rhythms in it and some clear, broad and ambitious beauty. Horus could not even understand what instruments were used to perform these pulsating and flying melodies. Bright figures were moving in all directions around and inside the translucent vimana in the rhythm of the music. They moved up and down, coming closer to each other and separating again as if it were some kind of game, or maybe it was a kind of dance or a form of communication. Horus noticed that that the flow of the same luminous figures is moving toward the nearest star, and part of it is already moving back. It reminded him of some kind of pilgrimage. But Horus wondered to which of gods this flow moved to?

As soon as he thought about it, he at once found himself next to the same radiant figure that he recently saw nearby. Horus had no doubts anymore, he folded his arms and said: 'Greetings, lord Osiris!'

The eyes of this extraordinary being looked right at him. Horus felt something very familiar in them. In a moment he remembered that exactly the same look had a stranger who spoke with him after that night, full of heavy despair when Horus was returning to the body and lay crumpled under the earth's weight. That time he helped him to recover, he eased his suffering. He whom Horus took for Osiris, as if seeing that Horus remembered and recognized him, just as then, leaving the mouth motionless as if to say with just a thought, he said: 'Greetings to you, my son.'

For a moment Horus felt dizzy out of joy. So it seemed to him even though he knew that he was far away from his body. But god himself responded to him! This inspired him: 'Let me thank you for your help and mercy! I did not say that the last time...'

The shining image remained absolutely motionless, but Horus heard the answer: 'Self-realized help those who ascend selflessly.' 'I'll never forget this. Permit me to ask, master.'

The divine image remained silent, and Horus realized that he could continue: 'What kind of ship is this, o lord, and who are these people?' 'These are the spirits of people who remember that their homeland is Space. Often at night, while their bodies are asleep, they come here to remember the forgotten and to learn new things. The ship of the subtle matter of thoughts was built by them. They still do not know how to use the power of spirit to move around in the universe without ships.'

Horus understood the meaning of what was said; it turned out that he probably was even praised because he came here himself without any devices, even without performing the rite in the great pyramid as it was before. But he did not know how it happened, and rightly believed that he cannot do it yet: 'I've seen your divine appearance recently on the Earth, but now I see you here. So, it is possible to move so fast?'

'Yes, you can move instantly to the speed of thought. Those who have mastered it can be in several places simultaneously.'

Horus was surprised: 'Only the gods can do that. But is it possible for people?'

The answer was even more surprising: 'You yourself are now in the earthly body on the Earth and at the same time you are here.'

Horus recalled that yes, just recently he was with the Hierophant: 'And how can one make yourself present in different places at once?'

'The Oneness penetrates the whole universe and is present everywhere at once. Being in you It is inextricably linked with It in all other beings. Therefore the image on the Earth which you saw was similar to the image that you see here.'

'Was it not your appearance, o lord? Don't you say that my spirit is similar to you?' 'Truly, the small is similar to the great. We only need to manifest the Oneness in us.'

'But only the gods can do that. Can people ever learn it?' asked Horus. 'Everything is possible by the growth of the spirit, my son.' It was just what inspired Horus the most: 'Thank you, Lord, for your wisdom and help!'

Then Horus could not resist and finally asked again: 'How to achieve a better growth of the spirit?'

The answer turned out to be quite a surprise for him: 'Think about how to understand compassion. True compassion is not in the feelings but in selfless help...'

Horus did not have time to once again thank the god. He almost immediately found himself back in the same room next to Hierophant. Horus stood up, bowed low before him and humbly thanked him for a great lesson. Hept Saft's eyes shone even stronger and more wonderful than ever, as Horus saw it. Perhaps, he saw and knew everything that was happening so far away from here: 'Now you know the main secret, my son.' 'Thanks to your wisdom, o blessed teacher.' 'You've passed all the tests and therefore you are worthy to know.'

'Tell me, how to call this radiant image?' asked Horus.

'This, my son, can be opened to you only by the gods themselves, when the time comes...'

PART 5

33. The Temple of Sacrifice and Beauty

For long Horus pondered on the words about compassion. The more he thought, the more it was revealed to him. At first, he understood compassion as a quite normal natural phenomenon. If suddenly any child or elderly person fell next to him and asked about help he would immediately without hesitation ran to help them as would any other normal person. But the revelations he had received indicated that the true height of the spirit is based on compassion. This meant that the gods themselves help people on the basis of their compassion. It turned out that this simple feeling, which leads to the same, in his view, simple actions, permeated the entire universe and extended to all beings. It extended especially on the higher beings because the lower animals are not always able to express it. Consequently, it was particularly human compassion that indicated the extent of his spirituality. He began to understand that the more developed a person, the more actively he helps others. Discovering such seemingly simple things, Horus began to notice something that was constantly happening with his wise grandfather. People came asking Ra-Ta for help at any time of the day and sometimes even night. He would always immediately respond to them and often he would at once left everything and go to where he was called.

Horus first thought that his grandfather, famous throughout the whole country, goes to help his friends and acquaintances, who he had great many. Then, hearing the talks of guests, he began to realize that Ra-Ta likewise used to go helping those who he had never known or seen. After their return from Poseidonis Mayum together with the saved prisoners, who had been in slavery for nearly a quarter of century, with the elders and residents of their villages as well as with the priests and some black leaders have come home to Ra-Ta and sincerely thanked him for helping his countrymen. The farmers have brought a lot of different gifts to express their gratitude. But Ra-Ta, warmly welcoming them all, modestly said in response that he was only doing his duty with the help of the One and his friends from Aztlan. He flatly refused to accept gifts, saying that they had everything they need in the family and even more than necessary. He added that it was better to distribute the brought food and things among those who need them the most: the poorest, the sick and orphans. Horus had no doubt that his grandfather would do just that, but upon seeing this with his own eyes he involuntarily again remembered the words about the selfless care and compassion.

A few days later came a great joy for all their family. Together with a group of new settlers arrived Una with her parents. The houses for them were being built just nearby. Asmini and Rame already knew about Horus's desire to marry the girl and were very pleased with it. Rame even said that he almost resigned to the fact that he might have no grandchildren because priests very often did not marry. Asmini, on the contrary, believed that her son with such fine and sensitive soul can love wholeheartedly and sooner or later would find his destiny. Una's parents were also happy. They had very warm attitude toward Horus and considered him their son. They often visited one another to talk. Horus tried his best to help with the construction, and in the evenings he and Una would go for a walk and discussed with each other all the most important questions. Una would tell what happened during this time in Alta, and Horus was talking about how he tried to understand the advice about compassion. Eventually he came to the conclusion that the best way for him to start to fulfill the supreme advice would be to just begin to help his wise grandfather who helped a great many people. People used to come to his grandfather to resolve difficult disputes when elders did not know which side should be supported, and Ra-Ta had to perform the duties of a judge. Often people came for support when there was a terrible sorrow, and he had to summon all his wisdom to show them the way out. But more often than any came those who suffered and needed recovery.

There were new diseases, physical and mental, they were caused by either a huge number of migrants or by large changes in the life of the country, and may be by both or some other causes unknown for the common people. Seeing that the stream of those who were in need of such assistance was increasing day by day, Ra-Ta decided to devote most of his time to them. Having learned about it, Horus and Una immediately volunteered to help him with what they could. The sage decided that since the house could no longer accommodate all the suffering people, they should do their job in the temple, where the patients used to come for help. He said that in the future it would be necessary to build new temples, and he even invented a name for them: it would be temples of Sacrifice and Beauty. Sacrifice, because people need to be taught to sacrifice their attention to the One, and Beauty because with the recovery of the spirit the body is also refining and thus becomes even more beautiful.

Horus and Una tried to be always with Ra-Ta. They listened how he conducts his ministry. A lot of people were arriving, many of them looked sick and weak. There were many crippled and people who were clearly disordered both bodily and spiritually. Ra-Ta calmly surveyed all the gathered, who usually did not fit inside the temple. Therefore the conversation had to be taken outside its walls: he was standing on the steps and people were sitting on the ground and listened.

Ra-Ta was not going to give the abstract sermons. On the first day, after a few general words about the fact that the Oneness pervades everything and that it is in every being, and that the duty of a human is to realize and manifest this, which is the first aid for the health and happiness, he then moved on to specific people and suggested: 'Let all those in need speak out right now.'

All those who came to him began to step out. Each had different troubles: one complained that his hands grew badly from his childhood, he was an invalid; the other had aching entrails; the third was always restless and all the while he was tossing and moaning. He also along with the others went to the sage, who was standing on the steps and briefly explained the essence of his troubles. Ra-Ta said, referring to both them and all the others: 'The Oneness helps everyone, but to get Its response it is necessary to consciously appeal to It. You all go to temples and see the gods. But how do you all imagine them? Now sit down here,' he spoke to those who had come up to him, pointing to the stairs. They sat on the steps.

'Close your eyes and think how you imagine all the god in the One, or you can imagine the Oneness through each god separately, because each of them is a particle of the unity. Imagine him, think of him, ponder and try to see him right in front of you in the most beautiful and majestic appearance.'

Besides those who got up on the steps, all the rest, who sat down on the ground, also closed their eyes and began to focus. This went on for some time and then the silence was broken, and all the present took their turns to talk. Although this entire experience lasted no more than twenty minutes, somebody said that his pain subsided. He who was too anxious, prayed to the gods for peace, and he said that he was able to calm down a little bit. Others also shared their impressions one at a time. But one girl, turning to the old man, said: 'I do not know how to imagine god. They are being drawn so different and I do not see them well.'

Ra-Ta noticed that it was something wrong with her eyes. Perhaps she had poor eyesight. He asked her: 'My daughter, who do you love the most in the world?'

The girl thought for a moment and said: 'Most of all I love the little son of my elder brother. He is a very cheerful child, very playful, and we always play with him and go for a walk together.

'In this case,' Ra-Ta continued his thought, 'Try to close your eyes and focus again. You can imagine the face of your older brother's son, but in your mind you should remember that god is in him, because when each of the gods incarnated on Earth, he was also a child. It was quite possible that one of them looked like your brother's son. But that's not the point. The point is your thought should appeal to the highest, to the One, to what we, humans, call God. After all, to get assistance even from your own grandfather you have to first call him. Then God will respond in you and his strength begins to guide you and to heal. This is the only way a person can achieve happiness in this life, for everything else, everything external cannot give him happiness, but rather is a cause of concern, labor and hassle. Happiness only dwells within, and it is there only in those people who have come to know what is the Oneness and the highest.

Having said that, Ra-Ta uttered the word with which he like all other priests and people of his nation would always end his prayer: 'Amen.' The dark-skinned old man who was sitting on the steps of the temple directly in front of him, asked: 'Wise Ra-Ta, you say amazing things! My heart tells us that it is all true. Tell me, blessed, why do you, Arians, always say the word Amen at the end of your prayers? What does it mean?'

Ra-Ta smiled: '"Amen" is the oldest and true name of the One or highest God, who is being served by other gods and the people, living and abiding in Him. In the language of our ancestors "Amen" means each and all. It also means the most superior, that is God manifested in everything. At the end we just call on his name, testifying in His presence and asking for His help. The Holy Name is the manifestation of the Deity. My brothers-priests have many secrets, which they should not reveal under pain of death. But the main secrets may be open to all; the life itself teaches us to worship the Deity of the Holy Name in the temple of our hearts. And when we become good friends with the One, the life is also changing for us. Previously we were in need of help, but now we can help others. A man who has realized the highest becomes like the sun — it illuminates the whole world and does not need to be illuminated from outside.

Horus and Una also heard the words of wise Ta-Ra, and Horus was amazed how deep was the wisdom of his own grandfather, whom he loved so much, and for who he could agree on anything. But he never asked his grandfather the most basic and important questions that these poor and unfortunate people asked about. He was struck by how clearly and simply his grandfather talked about the greatest, the most important thing that was seemed clear and obvious for them, belonging to priestly order by birth. These topics should necessary be contemplated upon in internal reflections; they were not supposed to say about these things in prayers, therefore no one talked about it, about the very essence of the concept of highest. Ra-Ta was talking simply, confidently and clearly, as a wise man of experience, who has realized it all by himself in his life and has become convinced in immutable reality the highest in everyone's life.

After the first conversation, that was so surprising to many, but nevertheless useful, Ra-Ta together with Horus and Una who helped him in his work, began to divide people by writing their names and the questions each of them had brought. Then they fixed a day and time for each person to come next time. Everyone was supposed to carry out certain procedures prior to their appointment, everyone was given some prescriptions. Someone had to abstain from food; someone else on the contrary was too exhausted, he had to eat normally; someone was recommended to constantly spend all his time in prayer; someone was suggested to walk more in the fresh air and commune with nature. And then on the appointed day everyone had to come once again to the temple to show what condition he was in and to be interviewed individually, to be treated and to participate in a joined prayer.

Days passed one after the other, week after week, month after month, the seasons changed one another. Nile overflowed and returned to its shores, people were ripping the harvest. But Horus and all those who came to his grandfather's temple were surprised to see the changes. Those who only two or three months ago had a sickly look, became normal and healthy. Parts of their body, arms and legs, which used to be sick before were getting healthy and filled up with energy; their eyes changed and emanated the light of joy and spirituality. Many of those who were sick got healed, their mood as well as their attitude to life were steadily changing. They ceased to be weak-willed victims, they ceased to be sufferers.

Although not all issues have been resolved: someone was still feeling pain or experiencing some other residual problem, but compared to the huge burden which they already got rid after applying the wisdom of Ra-Ta, which in his own words did not belong to him, the remaining minor problems did not frighten them and did not cause despair that they felt before. Ra-Ta, it seemed, had the wisdom of humanity. It was the wisdom collected by all previous generations of priests, sages and prophets. So as a result of implementing this knowledge people were proud with what they have achieved, they were happy and joyful. Their life has changed, they have become other people and it reflected in their eyes. They began to relate in a different way and act differently. Now they could manage their lives and could benefit their brothers who were in the same need as they a few months ago.

Horus never doubted the reality of higher phenomena and their omnipotence. This was evident for him from the very childhood. But he could not imagine that such deep and obvious results that can occur with the most common and unfortunate people. Horus was as amazed and surprised as parishioners and patients who took help from his grandfather, and sometimes he proudly thought that he also was involved in this great and good work of his grandfather. However, the word "pride" was hardly suited his inner state. With a simple quiet joy he just modestly stated and admitted to himself that he also played a small role in it, and he could help his grandfather in such a great cause — to serve his fellow man, to heal their bodies and souls.

Horus remembered every phrase that said his grandfather. Although he couldn't say how long his grandfather would live and when he would leave them, but he knew that when the time would come and Ra-Ta would go from this world, he would have to become his successor. He would have to do all those things that his grandfather could not do; to receive all those who came late and did not meet Ra-Ta: all those new ones who are still far away, or who do not even know about them and have not yet found the way to them.

At such moments Horus mentally thanked the gods for giving him such a good memory. Nevertheless, every time upon returning home Horus wrote down every word of his grandfather, every word of those who came to him and how wise Ra-Ta answered them. 'Let it be saved for future generations,' thought Horus. 'After all, I also some day will become old and leave this world. I will not be able to tell it to everyone. There will be people who will live after us. Let them also know and read such a great and simple wisdom that a human can understand in the world and transform his life.'

34. The Last Council in Peos

On this night the leaders of the twelve clans of the powerful northern part of Atlantis, who worshiped dark gods, gathered together for the last time in the same large and luxurious room.

The oldest, dressed in dark red and seated on the throne, said: 'All of you know that the children of sun gods have already begun to send their people to the land of their brothers. We also should start a full resettlement of our people. It is already a quarter of a century since we at this council decided to move to other lands to prevent our enemies from doubling their military might with the help of people from other countries. But now we cannot prevent them, many of them have moved to new lands. And if we go there, they will come out against us together with the local leaders and their soldiers. That time many years ago it seemed wise to just go to other lands in order to avoid this. But since then a lot was changed: our brave leaders Tuahell and Azeyotl were killed. The local savages resisted us with the fury of wild beasts, but the most important thing was that a local climate was much colder than what we were accustomed to in our island. We had to heat our homes for almost six months unlike our native land where we were happy with any coolness. Therefore many of those who departed have then returned back, and those who stayed are ready to come back at any time. So let us think together: what do we do next, considering that we have almost no time now.

The sage came down from the throne and come up to the wall of the hall in the form of a large and relief map lighted from above and below. The map displayed all the countries of the world along with the seas and oceans: 'We need to decide what we will choose now. Should we go again to the North-East (shows British Peninsula) with all our forces? Or should we go through Mayapan (shows the Yucatan and the Isthmus with Poseidonis) or to the valley of the Great River (shows Egypt)? Or should we divide so that a group of us would go into the land of Myra and in the land of Fire and Metal (pointing to the west and the east of North America), and the other group would go to the shores of a large Middle lake the (pointing to the north of the Mediterranean)? Let each leader decide his fate.

Another old man, dressed in black, gets up: 'Most of the Solar gods' sons are moving to Mayapan and to the valley of the Great River. I think we do not need to go there. If they unite with the local tribes, then it will be hard for us to beat them all and many of our people will die in battle with them. I also see no sense in going to the land of

Myra and to the land of Fire and Metal (pointing to the west and the east of North America). It is also as cold there as on the opposite shores of the ocean.'

Balamantu rises and says: 'We should not divide in such a difficult and dangerous hour. And we should not fight the enemies now when their number may double. We have only one option: to lead all our people to the northern shores of the great Middle lake. There are still not many migrants from Alta there, and the climate there is only a bit cooler than in our native Poseidonis. We must be there before them. When we get a foothold there we can then move on to the east and to the south to fight our enemies and eventually defeat them!'

Another member of the Board gets up: 'Wisely said, Balamantu! In this case all the new land along with countless new slaves would be ours!'

All participants support this decision. They approach the map and put their hands together at the specified location.

The oldest says: 'If this is the will of the gods, it is time for all of us to lead our soldiers to war! We should start without delay tomorrow at dawn. In the morning together with our people we will gather at the port and begin to send troops. And may gods of the Moon help us!'

Everyone repeats the last phrase: 'May gods of the Moon help us!' and begin to break up.

35. The Volunteer Corps

Pharaoh and his advisers came to the mirror. In it through the fog they began to see a distant unknown country. They saw a high hill with a beautiful temple on it and a crowd of armed men standing on the ground in front of the temple on the top of the hill. At the bottom as far as eyes could see there was a great sea of people that filled the entire city to its distant shores on the horizon, where it was bordered with a blue strip of the real sea. All the streets nearest to the center were crowded with carts with food supplies. Pharaoh and his advisors carefully peered into the group of people standing on a platform at the top of the hill. One of them stood out. He wore the armor of glittering bronze. When everyone's attention riveted on him, the image has become larger and his figure and eyes became better visible. His eyes glowed with a fire of courage and determination, and a huge crowd was waiting at the bottom. His very appearance radiated power and strength and all those who were observing it from a distant Egypt realized that he was the chief or king. He looked attentively at the area and understood that everyone was waiting for his words. Then he came up to the edge of the temple square and began to speak and a resonant echo carried his words. The observers of this event including Pharaoh could not understand how such a huge mass of people could hear everything, but by the movements and reaction of the crowd they realized that the words of the leader reached even to the farthest rows. His language was beautiful and unknown and at first the hearers could not catch the meaning of his words. The magical mirror did its job and after a while they began to understand the words of the leader of the unknown distant country. His words started to sound in their head in their own language. At least, they began to understand the general meaning: 'They broke into the house of our distant neighbors at night like the robbers, they took over the whole country and many Iberian kings were forced to serve them. They do not ask for permission, they go and take someone else's property, consider it their own, and they think that all others are only their slaves. In their arrogance they know no one but themselves, they do not know anything about other nations, they do not feel that our earth is blooming with prowess throughout the county around a great Mediterranean lake. They do not know that no Greek would agree to live on his knees. What do they know? They know only themselves and those who are afraid of them? So now let them see us and feel the strength of our soldiers! Let all people know — the oracle of Apollo, the Sun-god, announced that the gods of Olympus would grant the victory to the Greeks and to all our allies! Let their will be fulfilled! We're setting out today in order to meet the enemy before he comes to the lands of our friends! Let's hit the road, warriors! All gods are with us!'

Cries of thousands of people echoed powerfully and booming in the distance. The leader came down from the hill and first marched west toward the sunset. A huge crowd uniformly and orderly followed him.

The more Pharaoh and his advisers looked at this army, the more surprised they became with how armed they were; they had conventional weapons: spears, swords, arrows, shields, and other creations of artisans and blacksmiths, just as his army. 'How can they withstand the battle against rods of lightning and vimanas?' asked in bewilderment all those who were watching the marching of the distant army in the magic mirror, but they could not find any answer to this question. The conventional weapons forged by mere mortals cannot resist the gifts of the gods and wise magicians. People will not be able to withstand such an unequal and terrible battle. How else can one imagine its inevitable outcome? But however these distant witnesses thought all they could do was to wait. And they had to wait for many more days to see everything with their own eyes...

36. The Death of Poseidonis

Supreme Ruler of Alta gathered his council of senior priests and his chief aides. Everyone knew that the deadline has approached, but only he could give the order. King had been long lost in thought but then he said: 'Get ready. Convey my order to all: arise you, the people of good law and cross this land while it is dry. The lords of black-faced will survive only for one more night and two days on this patient land. They are condemned and should be overthrown along with it. The spirits of elements obey to the will of the dark sorcerers, and though they cannot stop the spirits of underground fire, let all the people of the open eye inflict the state of slumber on them. Let even they escape the pain and suffering.'

The king with shining face rose from his turquoise throne and continued. He was obviously quite worried: 'I order all my soldiers to seize the vimanas of all the sons of Thevetat and his followers.'

Then he appealed to the Las-lu: 'Immediately send a unit of soldiers with the best of our magicians. You know their main center in Peose. All the vimanas should be taken and returned. In order to prevent them from stopping you, you should use subtle powers and immerse them in dream. We don't have time anymore.'

Las-lu bowed his head in respect: 'Yes, master.' 'Do it now,' ordered the king.

Las Lu retired. The king addressed to all gathered: 'Now it's time. You go and prepare your people. We will set off just after the sunset.'

The participants quickly dispersed. Everyone's faces were all tense and stern. Everyone knew what was going on. King was left alone in the big hall; only at the bottom of the window stood his wife and looked into the distance. He came down from his throne and approached her. Silently they gazed at the landscape of their native island. The woman had tears in her eyes. King touched her shoulder and said: 'It's time.'

The queen kept looking. She whispered: 'Goodbye, my beautiful land. Farewell! Let your long sleep be peaceful. And when you re-ascend from the abyss then we will see you again.'

Tears ran down her cheeks, and the king's eyes filled with tears, too, he could not hold them back. Then they both turned and left.

The landing that was moving in the direction of Peos landed just after sunset. All the vimana devices enhancing mental orders of the white magicians were switched on. The whole area was submerged in a dream. All the vimanas of the night worshipers were assembled and delivered in half an hour to the lord of Alta. They carried those who went on a long journey across the ocean: to the Pyrenees and in the valley of the Great River.

All the rest, the majority of the population, had to walk on an isthmus on the newly built road. People also started to move after sunset. A huge crowd flowing like a vast river, incorporating streams from all the other towns and villages and increasing along its way, flowed smoothly into the darkness to the borders of their home country. The leading units of the column soon came to the isthmus. The road was wide and there was enough space for everyone. People carried whatever they could take — carts, children and animals. All were silent and depressed.

The procession lasted all night. Streams of people kept

coming and coming. The most of vimanas, except for the last group of Alta ruler and his entourage, have already reached distant lands in the east, but people kept going. The great river of Aztlan people flowed into Mayapan and according to previous arrangements each group moved from the main road to the appointed place, where they were waited for in their new home: new villages, places and new cities.

The lords of the dark will or as they were called, the people of Aztlan, Thevetata's sons, slept peacefully suspecting nothing. Some of them woke up just before dawn with the sound of thunder. The rest went on to sleep. Those who awoke were surprised: the thunder came not from the sky and from under the ground. They looked out the window and saw a terrible picture: glowing streams of meteors were falling in the night dark sky like fire arrows. They hit the ground raising the firestorm, dust and fog. Others fell far away from the island into the sea, raising a cloud of spray. It seemed that the earth itself was in motion.

Those who awoke could not wake up the rest despite it was already daylight, and they decided to act. Jumping into the yard and on the street they could not find their vimanas what astonished them even more. The understanding that something incorrigible had happened overwhelmed them but it was too late, they could not do anything. The volcanoes of Poseidonis woke up one after the other. With a deafening roar and letting up monstrous clouds of smoke and dust the volcanoes scattered melted pieces of stone and earth in all directions.

The agony did not last long. The terrible surf caused by either meteorites or by lowering of the island — those who were still alive could not understand it — flooded the cities one after another. The storm which raged in the air was increasingly making its way in the water as well. With the terrible onslaught the waves demolished houses; they not just flooded them, they just tore them on their way and leveled them to the ground, mixed with mud, fish and algae.

The last thousands of people of the millions who have crossed the Isthmus and deepened further in the new opens of Mayapan by the new road first heard this roar behind them. As soon as they stepped on the land of the peninsula and looked back, they saw that the isthmus was also flooded by the waves and the roadside stones were scattered to the sides. The land here also went under the water. The night lights illuminating the road continued to flicker under the water, but even the last groups of people were saved.

Nobody could say who was late, who could not leave the house, who followed behind. They could find it out only after their settlement. But even there in spite of the management and the presence of mind of those who were receiving the newcomers among the newly arrived reigned general confusion and depression. Only there it was possible to find out who was where. And even there those who could not find their loved ones retained a faint hope that their relatives and friends might go with another group, or that they could be in different part of the stream or go to another village or another town. They still had to search and find all those who survived. Only in case of failure they could take as lost or dead all those who did not escape.

This battle of wind and water against the land lasted all the next day, the next night and the following day. The land fell under their onslaught, and by the beginning of the third morning at the site of what was once called Aztlan there was only sticky and squelched water with whirlpools and waves wandering in all directions mixed with mud and the remains of plants and trees.

37. The Battle

At dawn Ra-Ta knocked at the door of the grandson's room. Horus did not sleep, although the sun had just risen above the horizon. He jumped out of bed and greeted his grandfather.

'Horus, need your help,' said Ra-Ta.

Hearing this phrase from Ra-Ta only for the second time in his life Horus was overjoyed: surely he can help his grandfather. 'I'm glad to help you, grandfather,' he said.

Grandfather calmly added: 'Not me, Horus, but you should help right now. Come on.'

They went into his room. Ra-Ta sat down, his grandson sat next to him. Then, the old man said: 'Concentrate and follow me.'

The concentration was the usual state for Horus and it did not cause any difficulties. After collecting his thoughts and his mind together, Horus saw himself as if from above. This happened before but that before it was vague. Now he saw clearly as he had nothing to do with this body sitting next to him. And just in the same way his grandfather was sitting next to him. Rather, it was also the grandfather's body, because Ra-Ta himself was hovering above it in the form of a radiant being, which was not very distinct and gradually changing its shape. When Horus realized what was happening, his grandfather told him only one sentence: 'Come with me.'

Then he instantly saw a huge space, the beach beneath it, and boundless distances of the Middle Lake. Then he saw the opposite bank and at the bottom was a huge camp with the soldiers who just woke up. The first rays of the sun barely touched their tents. The soldiers whose race he didn't know had just risen from sleep and were preparing for the upcoming battle.

Horus was surprised not only at this instantaneous movement, he was even more surprised at what he had tried to understand before but now begun to see it so easily and clearly. He could call it the breath of the stars or stellar mildew or dust which descends from the sky. It was something he sometimes noticed in the form of a subtle phenomenon in the world, invisible for others. He did not even know what to call it. It was neither a matter, nor a thought and nor sounds. It was something like rays, but not like rays of the sun or moon, which clearly shine and make objects visible. These rays fell differently. They were like rain. With its smooth motion they were reminiscent of sinking dust, but yet they didn't look like dust.

Sometimes in his normal waking state Horus felt their presence, he even thought that he was starting to see them, and then he remembered in his heart the states that he had experienced there, far above. They seemed to bring him back to that state. But best of all he was able to feel it only once, when he stood in front of the temple, and the sun was already setting. A bright ray of the red sun lit the temple walls from behind the distant mountains and at the same time all around was the sinking into the darkness. When the sun finally set, and the lights in front of the temple were lit, this contrast increased even more: the dark blue sky, the stars that were visible on it until the moon came up, and reddish lights of the temple, built of pale yellow stone. At that moment, standing on the plates, he seemed to see again these descending rays. He did not even know what to call them. These were not rays, they didn't look like rays, but that day as today he had no words to define them. And then he began to call them simply, just for himself: the spirit of the stars.

And now again he saw this spirit of the stars which was like frost or poplar fluff. It was coming top-down and quietly set on faces and shoulders of these unknown people. They were strange distant warriors, whom he had never seen or even heard of their nationality. He knew that the northern shores of the Middle or the Mediterranean lake, as it was also called, were inhabited by completely different people, who spoke other languages. And now he saw their soldiers, he saw their brave faces, their peaceful and grim determination when they were putting on their armor and collecting weapons, ready to go into battle. And he was surprised to see that this spirit of the stars is setting down at them as if blessing them, as if preparing them for what would take place. Or maybe it was showing to him how to understand what was happening. Horus already understood: 'If this phenomenon occurs here, then these people must be great heroes.'

Then Horus remembered his grandfather. He saw that Ra-Ta was beside him. Suddenly, their attention was drawn by the sound of martial horns. The first horn resounded relatively close of them, then followed the other one from a more distant place. The warriors, who have already put on armor and taken up the arms, were quickly coming out of their tents moving somewhere down, where their troops were gathering. Horus saw an unknown commander, whose appearance radiated extraordinary courage and determination. Following his orders detachments were built and arranged one behind the other. They were increasing in number.

Following his grandfather, Horus, invisible to all,

looked at what's going on ahead of him. There, far away, he saw a vast plain. Further, closer to the shores of the Middle Lake he saw a line of other people. When his attention was directed there, that place seemed to become closer and he noticed there another army that was being arranged. The soldiers were equipped with the other kind of armor. They were taller and more powerful. Each of them left an impression of a powerful and strong person. They also had their own commanders.

Further to the west behind them in the distance Horus saw a great number of ships moored to the shore. But it was a different side of the land, it was not the shore of the Middle lake, it was the shore of the external larger sea. Horus saw a huge number of soldiers in the direction of west and east and thought, 'How hard it would be to fight such an army!'

Meanwhile, from above, where they mentally transported from recently, he heard the sounds of horns and pipes. He looked back and saw the first army, which he saw at the beginning. Orderly arrayed, glittering with weapons and armor, the army was coming down the plain towards the warriors of other army, who left their ships, lined up and moved towards them. The distance was not very big. The sun had risen only slightly over the horizon and lit everything around with the morning light. The first rows of the two hostile armies already drew close to each other and released their missiles into the air. The army that moved from above threw darts and shot arrows, and the one that came from below from the sea threw stones and waved over heads with some device, which Horus had never seen before.

But it did not last long. The last hundred steps that separated the two armies were quickly passed. And there two powerful nations, who came from different places and met on this plot of land, were faced in direct combat. Then Horus heard the roar of such power that he rarely heard. Simultaneous strikes of thousands of swords against each other and against shields and armor, furious cries of the advancing warriors or cries of pain of the wounded — all mixed up in one big and discordant tumult and surrounded him on all sides.

He recalled for a moment his feelings when, being at the top, he remembered about the Earth and heard a terrible roar beneath. What was happening now was obviously similar. Although he saw the difference also. In the air he sensed the fury and rage that would be difficult to catch from afar. Again he remembered about his grandfather and saw that his grandfather was hovering over the heads of soldiers in the front rows going from above. And he decided to go to him and help. Horus positioned himself next to his grandfather, and then he saw that what he called a spirit of the stars was coming from his formless and semi-bright cloud as well as from his grandfather — it was coming from them down on the warriors. Horus was trying to understand what was happening. He thought: 'Maybe it comes down on us, accumulates, and then we pass it down further?' Together with his grandfather they gave the power of stars to the soldiers, especially to those who fought in the front ranks.

The fierce battle at a great distance, which was immeasurable by steps or by view, unfolded more and more until not a single spot of land remained empty. There was not a single sound that would not be involved in it, no thought, no other feeling — everything was boiling in the war.

Horus and his grandfather continued to move over the rows of brutally fighting soldiers. Sometimes he saw clear pictures, sometimes the pictures blurred in front of him. He seemed to become disconnected. Sometimes his eyes turned upward and he saw hovering birds in the sky, looking for something above the battling armies. He could not say how long did it last. Perhaps, the battle continued for not very long, not for all day. At the same time he could not measure the time and could not understand how much of it had passed. The troops that came down from above clearly afflicted those who were below, despite the fact that not all their army was ready for a fight; some of the warriors were still disembarking the ships, forming, and after putting their weapons and their ranks in order they moved towards the enemy.

The furious battle that raged all around and fully penetrated the consciousness of Horus, though he managed to stay an independent observer, took place for no apparent reason. The only thing he could understand after some time, which conditionally might be called a few hours, he could see that despite the bottom army was getting reinforcement the soldiers that moved from above were pressing the enemies that came from the sea pushing them back to the sea and to their ships. The army descended from above was also getting reinforcements. Those units that were either far away from the main camp or were only approaching or were located somewhere else — they also appeared from afar and drew near to the site of a grand battle to engage in it along with everyone.

Some time later Horus began to understand what was going on around him. The outcome of the battle became more or less clear to him, although obviously it was still very far away from the end and it hardly even reached its midpoint. He saw how the troops of the army that descended from above could oust the alien forces closer to the sea and back to their ships. Horus now realized that the warriors below were uninvited guests. Several times Horus tried to understand what kind of army opposed from the bottom. He did not know much about the nationality of the first army, so he could not understand, who what nation the second army belong to. Outwardly, they were more like the people of Aztlan, but what he saw on the streets of Alta had very little to do with them. The only thing that could be seen was their height and complexion. Although the color of their skin was slightly darker and the bodies were stronger.

On the other hand, he was not used to see armed Aztlan men because neither Iltar nor Wotan had these maces, these huge shields, these shiny helmets. Horus had never seen it, but gradually he began to understand that, apparently, it was indeed the army of Aztlan, but it was not the army. Rather, this army was not from the part of the Aztlan where Horus had been. They were not soldiers of Alta, but probably the soldiers of Peos, from where his grandfather could rescue the kidnapped prisoners.

All these thoughts distracted Horus's attention for a while. Sometimes he absorbed in himself but then he would come back to the reality that was unfolding around him trying to understand what was happening. He saw that the top army began to thrust the strangers even more, the latter ranks of which were already close to the waterfront to where new ships were constantly coming to put new units ashore.

And at some moment of the battle when the sun was nearing the zenith and was high in the sky, through the deafening noise, the roar and fury of battle, Horus heard some other noise. It was incredible noise that he had never heard or imagined. It was as if the earth itself tremored from some unknown distance, from under the ground, from under the sea which was also located on the ground. It was as if the land under the sea started to groan and rattle. Horus was at first very surprised. He felt no fear but only tried to understand, but still he did not understand.

After a while this terrible noise subsided, very high in the sky appeared many brilliant birds. When Horus looked closer at them he realized that those were not birds but vimanas. And there were quite a lot of them. 'What are they doing here?' Horus thought. 'Maybe they came to participate in the battle?' However, the vimanas rapidly swept over the battling parties like a sign and continued their way. They did not take any part in the battle. Horus heard the words as if coming from the sky spoken in some unknown language and just understood their meaning, though no word was known to him. The voice from the sky ordered to someone: 'Withdraw your troops!'

A few minutes later Horus realized that something was happening on the battlefield. The battle itself seemed to slow down; the contact points between the armies began to separate. The above army stopped their attack and ceased to push the army below, which retreated to the ships where it formed and rearranged as if for a next fight. At the same time, the farthest units of the upper army after surpassing the opponent were returning back as if by the order of their commander. Upon returning they formed again and, pointing their spears at the enemy beneath them, they waited for further orders.

At this time the terrible rumble repeated. It resembled an underground thunder of incredible length, everything was shaking. Horus wasn't present here in his physical body, he did not feel the shaking, but he sensed it, and he did see it: ships standing near the shore, the soldiers themselves, those who descended from the ships and those who stood in the first ranks — everything was shaking and moving in an unknown direction, and the roar grew. Then he saw what was going on behind the ships. He saw a huge blue wall covered with foam and spray sparkling in the sun. This wall was directly behind the army of aliens.

Before Horus could understand what it was or even to become surprised, he heard new rumble, thunder, crackling and gritting fused together. Near the place of disembarking he saw that the earth diverged with cracking, rumbling and squeaking. He could not even describe the sounds that accompanied it. While the emerged crack was being filled with water, the huge wall of blue water covered with foam and spray made it to the shore. He saw alien ships shot up like frightened birds, and then the beach shot up, too, but on the contrary that part of it which was cracking before turned and began to roll like an overturned table. The army, which was forming and to be ready for further protection, all these countless units of armed soldiers — all mixed up in the air with earth, water, foam, spray and muddy streams of dirt. It seemed this terrifying movement was carrying everything to the sky and stirring at the same time. This continued for a while. Then the flow turned and under the gravity dashed down with all its mass. A new wave, this time flying down, mixed with vehicles, people, weapons, fragments of sails, trees, plants, grass, earth, water, mud, rocks, and god knows what else, fell down like a giant surf coming from sky right in front of Horus's eyes.

And only then he remembered about the army which was on the top and which had been ordered to retreat. Turning to that side Horus saw that there was neither a plain nor a shore; it was only sea. 'What happened to these heroes?' he thought and felt that his grandfather thought the same. They quickly shifted to where just recently there was the upper army that could retreat only a little bit. And when they found a new edge of boiling water that was foaming and pouring on the beach, they saw the beach and could not understand what it consisted of; it looked like a cliff of mixed rocks. There they saw the remains of troops; the back rows of soldiers were hastily retreating back into the country to escape from the terrible disaster.

Horus bitterly realized that what was left was less than half of what he had seen before. He did not know what their loss in the battle was, but he realized that even if the victory was on their side, most of the heroic army of the victorious people was destroyed in the same way as were killed their enemies, who came uninvited to their land.

38. Sphinx and Toth

Ra-Ta and Horus stood on the roof of the temple and looked around. Sea water mixed with the water of the Great River filled the space as far as the eye could see. And Horus decided to ask his grandfather: 'Grandpa, how long will this flood continue?'

Ra-Ta gazed thoughtfully into the distance. Then he said: 'This time the water will soon subside. Before, when there were floods, it lasted for a long time. Now only the Nile overflowed because the sea water arriving from the north impedes its flow.

And then Horus decided to ask the questions he never asked his grandfather before. He somehow wanted to know right now at this dramatic and disastrous for the country moment, what would happen to it after. And he asked: 'Grandpa, what will happen to Egypt?' 'Don't you remember what your teacher of wisdom Toth told you?'

Horus thought... 'I remember, I then wanted to ask you. He said that other children would come in the land of Egypt and they would not believe in anything, neither in the soul nor in its life, that death would be more valuable to them.'

Then his unfailing memory that he had since childhood quietly revealed to him the content of the prediction. And as if reading some invisible book Horus began to recite before his grandfather. Although the text about the prediction was quite alarming and not very clear, Horus nevertheless was happy to once again show his grandfather that his studying was not vainly and that he may be worthy to be his grandson. And somewhere far away in a corner of his mind Ra-Ta noted to himself what a good grandson he had.

'O, Egypt, Egypt, your religion will become a mere fairy tale that your children, who will be destined to come in due time, will not believe in; nothing will remain but carved words, and only the stones will speak of thy piety. And on that day people will get tired of life, and they will cease to consider the Universe worthy of sacred admiration and worship... They will prefer darkness to light, they will find death more profitable than life, and no one will raise their eyes to the sky... As for the soul and faith in its immortal nature, and as for hopes to achieve immortality... they will deride all these and will even convince themselves of its falsity...'

And the gods will abandon mankind — what a terrible thing — and only evil angels will remain who will mingle with people and involve them, unfortunate, in all sorts of reckless crimes, war and looting, fraud and all the actions that are hostile to the soul's nature. Then the land will not be unshakable anymore... the sky will not keep the stars in their orbits and they will no longer follow their usual celestial ways... Then the old age will come down to the world. There will be no religion; everything will become messy and distorted; all good will disappear.

But when all this happens... then the One will look at everything and will deter the mess with Its will. It will cleanse the world of evil, wash it with floods, burn it with fierce fire, or walk through it with wars and pestilence. Thus It will return the world its former appearance so that the Cosmos could continue to be honored, worshipped and admired...

Such is the new birth of the cosmos, when everything becomes good again and the reverence for nature is restored; and it is done with the passage of time according to the eternal Supreme will...'

After Horus finished, for some time they were silent. Then Horus asked him: 'How long will it take for people to come back again to the knowledge of the Cosmos?'

The grandfather said: 'Only the most wise have all calculations. We can only know what we know.' 'Grandpa, what do we do when these days will come?'

Ra-Ta looked at the water-drenched horizon. 'Well, what can we do, Horus? We will come to the people then again. Again, we will be reminding them about the truth, about knowledge, about eternity.' 'I will also come with you, Grandpa,' said Horus. Ra-Ta looked at him and smiled. 'Yes, my boy. If you have the desire and courage you can always be with me wherever I go.'

They both fell silent and thoughtfully watched the idly running waves that reflected the sun. Then Horus looked at the face of Sphinx. It seemed to him that this face was looking at everything calmly and joyfully without any fear or anxiety, indicating that one day in the future this complex world subjected to calamities and horrors will be all right.

EPILOGUE

The rays of the sun shone in the waves. Ripples in the water formed cascades of light garlands that could be seen from the beach. A boy watched in fascination into the distance. Then he turned to his father and said: 'Dad, did you have a son that time?' The man adjusted his hat and looking at the midday sun, which already began to bake heavily, smiled and replied: 'No, Hugh. But then I had a good and very clever grandson who asked many interesting and important questions.'

The boy wondered and looked into the water trying to remember something.

At this time, they heard a woman's voice from afar: 'Edgar! Hugh-Lynn! It's dinner time!'

They both turned. She waved and went back into the house. The man got up shaking off the dust and said: 'Well, Hugh-Lynn? Mom is calling, come on.'

The boy jumped up quickly and nimbly, grabbed his father's outstretched hand, and together, talking quietly, they went home. Not only Mom and a younger brother were waiting for them, but also visiting relatives, who gathered in the living room for dinner.

2007-2013, Moscow.

Printed in Great Britain
by Amazon